# PALATABLE PANTRIES
# AND LAVISH LARDERS

A Complete Pantry Guide

*by*

Rhonda M. Mircovich

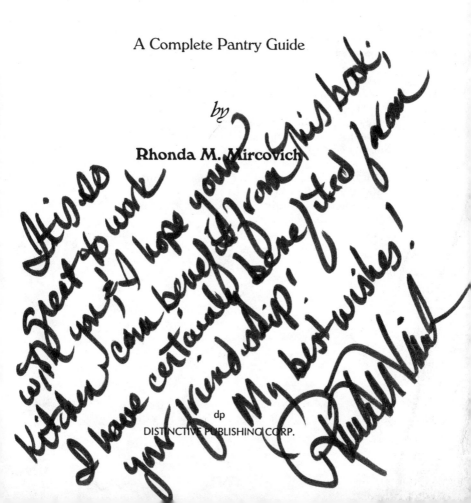

dp
DISTINCTIVE PUBLISHING CORP.

Palatable Pantries and Lavish Larders
By Rhonda M. Mircovich
Illustrations by Peggy Irvine
Copyright 1993 by Rhonda M. Mircovich

Published by Distinctive Publishing Corp.
P.O. Box 17868
Plantation, Florida 33318-7868
Printed in the United States of America

ISBN: 0-942963-33-4
Library of Congress No.: 92-30475
Price: $14.95


Library of Congress Cataloging-in-Publication Data

Mircovich, Rhonda M., 1958-
    Palatable pantries and lavish larders : a complete pantry guide / by Rhonda M. Mircovich.
        p.   cm.
    Includes bibliographical references and index.
    ISBN 0-942963-33-4 (tradesoft) : $14.95
    1. Kitchens—Planning. 2. Food. 3. Food—Storage.   I. Title.
TX655.M55   1992
641—dc20                                             92-30475
                                                         CIP

# Table of Contents

# ACKNOWLEDGMENTS

THIS BOOK HAS BEEN COMPILED during two years of research, developing, testing, and analysis. There have been innumerable cookbooks examined and cross referenced, along with FOOD AND DRUG ADMINISTRATION guidebooks, extension service pamphlets, home economist manuals, and kitchen help books. I should like to acknowledge especially:

*Secrets of Better Cooking,* 1973 READERS DIGEST

*Basic Foods,* June C. Gates

*Gourmet Magazine,* CONDÉ NAST PUBLICATIONS, INC.

*Handbook of Food Preparation,* AMERICAN HOME
   ECONOMISTS' ASSOCIATION

*Meal Management,* Kinder/Green

*Natures Incorporated,* Portland, Oregon

OREGON EXTENSION SERVICE

*Kitchen Book,* Terrence Conran, CROWN PUBLISHERS

*Kitchen Science,* Howard Hillman, HOUGHTON-MIFFLIN

*Kitchen Building Guide for Architects,*
   Patrick Galvin, STRUCTURES PUBLISHING

*Antique Household Gadgets and Appliances,*
   David de Haan, BARRONS PUBLISHERS

*Sunset Magazine,* SUNSET PUBLISHING CORP.

*Southern Living Cookbooks,* OXMOOR HOUSE

*Better Homes Cookbooks,* BETTER HOMES AND
   GARDENS

*LaRousse Gastronomique,* CROWN PUBLISHERS

*Victory at the Supermarket,* Joanne Coughran, LIVING
   BOOKS

*Spices of the World Cookbook,* McCormick, PENGUIN

My heartfelt acknowledgment and grateful appreciation go to my friends: Cheri Swoboda, home economist and writer for *Food Day Magazine*, Portland, Oregon, Peggy Irvine, artist extraordinaire, and to Denise Thorne for her diligent and patient efforts in the typing, correcting, and perfecting of this manuscript. I acknowledge, as well, the enthusiastic support of *all* of my friends.

For their enduring patience and unconditional support through the writing of this book, I should like to thank my family, Don, Nathan and Bonni Jeanne, to whom this book is dedicated.

In the acknowledgment which I wrote before going into production with this book, I thanked M.F.K. Fisher for her assistance and encouragement throughout the writing of this book. Now the gratitude must be declared posthumously. Along with millions of others who were her fans, I was saddened by her passing. She has left an enduring legacy for those who have and will experience her wonderful writings.

# INTRODUCTION

An ORGANIZED AND WELL STOCKED PANTRY or larder is the secret of all successful kitchens. This essential part of the kitchen is the resource on which you can depend, as you deal with the inevitable adjustments and accidents which occur while cooking. A pantry is the key foundation for all meal planning as well, whether it be for a lavish dinner party or for a nice, palatable meal for you and your family. Having a well stocked pantry involves more than being *prepared* to cook; it allows you to approach food preparation with a confidence that can positively affect all of your culinary results.

Whether you are a novice at cooking or a gastronomical expert, there are those days when the efforts of putting out a pleasurable meal can turn any sensible person into an unreasonable tyrant. The fact is, merely *following* a recipe can be difficult, without the frustration involved in putting together all of your efforts without snags or jags. Think of that last minute frenzy to find something in your cupboards to substitute for a missing ingredient which you thought you had, but now must dash out to the store to purchase! Did you ever say, at such moments, "There has to be a better way to cope with this"? There is. An organized pantry can provide the solution.

With a properly stocked *Basic Pantry* you will find yourself serving up dishes with less effort, less time consumed, and more enjoyment. You will discover that you can prepare more of your meals with a touch of flair, since the many frustrations involved in cooking will be alleviated, and you will be free to be more creative with your own culinary bent.

As your lifestyle and needs change, your pantry

may change too. In this book you will find chapters
that provide alternate pantry menus which will help
you meet those needs. The "Resource Guide" is your
pantry manual. Refer to it for information about the
uses, storage, and substitutions for a myriad of foods,
spices and herbs. Use this guide for the source of ideas
to make your cooking efforts more gratifying — as well
as accurate — and most important, better tasting. If you
begin with a *Basic Pantry,* your daily needs will be
much easier to meet; you can entertain without
anxiety and be ready for any occasion. You'll find that
the time you spend in the kitchen is *less* in time and
more in enjoyment.

# PALATABLE PANTRIES
# AND
# LAVISH LARDERS

# Chapter 1

## FOOD FOR THOUGHT:
## A BRIEF HISTORY OF THE
## PANTRY AND LARDER

FROM WHENCE DID THE NECESSITY for a larder
come? It came through progress! The early ancestors
of present day man had to cook and eat their meats as
soon as they were killed, in order to prevent quick-
spoiling meat from doing major damage to their lower
intestines. They didn't have dinner parties, so dinner
hour was just about any time food was ready and
available. This was necessarily so.

When people discovered the process for smoking
or drying meats, vegetables, and fruits in order to
preserve them, it became possible to hunt heavily and
then rest for a few days, storing foods until they were
needed.

Communal living — in the gastronomical as well as
economic sense — then became a wise endeavor. The
clustered families tried a "village store," where
everyone contributed to the bounty and shared in the
plentiful seasons as well as the periods of hunger
during droughts. Soon there were surpluses, which led
to trade among people who harvested or hunted or
created items which could be traded. Crafts, foodstuffs,
and services could be bartered.

It didn't take long for some individuals — because
they were able to accumulate more bargaining items
— to rise above the others. The birth of the class struggle

had begun. People came to realize that they must guard their wealth — at that time, primarily food and clothing — in order to have greater purchasing power. Money — purchasing power — in its various forms, came into being. Thus began civilization.

Centuries later, during the Middle Ages in central Europe, the first pantries — called armoires — were evolving. Man had come a long way, in terms of both foodstuffs and ways to cook them. Sharing victuals and rituals with travelers and countrymen became the most popular way to gain acceptance with people or to seal agreements of trade or truce. One aspect of this trade and travel was the many new spices, seasonings, and foods that became readily available — like salt, for example — which greatly increased the possibilities of flavor in food, as well as in storage and preservation. The people who managed to cook flavorful meals over an open fire were thankful for more ways to enhance — if not disguise — the tastes of foods. Finding a suitable place to store the spices, sugar, and dried fruits became a significant undertaking. A traveler would store such treasures in a small chest. Others used dark, cool rooms the size of large closets on the lower floors of their fortresses and castles, or used freestanding cupboards, hence the armoire.

As civilization progressed, the wealthy became more adept at serving lavish meals to their fellow royalists. They needed larger food storages with abundant quantities of fowl, game, vegetables and fruits. Out of this need came the birth of the larder, which was a large room, kept cool, for storing preserved meats, vegetables, and large quantities of staples.

As time marched on, Europe's gastronomical excesses kept in step with the rise and fall of many empires.

Meanwhile a new world was being discovered, and our colonial forefathers, facing difficult challenges in survival, grappled with the problem of providing food for their families. These courageous settlers, after unloading their ships of spices and tea, braved the elements to forge a place where they could flourish. They met and made peace with natives who sought to protect their land; the pilgrims fought against harsh weather and wild animals. Open fires were still the only means of cooking, and colonists huddled close to the coals in the frigid winters. They salted and smoked their foods for eating and storing in their rudimentary larders, while American Indians taught them about new edibles and herbs.

By the time of the Civil War, kitchens had become much more efficient. People were developing means of cooking with hot irons over fires. Western settlers fleeing the war — and later, seeking gold — had to pack their wagons for the long journey with a small, but beneficial larder. Once they settled their land and set up homesteads, the need for plentiful supplies in their traveling wagons was still crucial, due to the long distances between their home and the nearest squatter or township. Finally, the war ended, and the country got on with the business of being, truly, the *United States of America*.

By the 20th century, the pace of change had escalated; staffs of the wealthy were busy assisting the mistress of the home with regular entertaining. Even the middle classes could afford help. The larger kitchens often had dressers and cabinets in them to store the vast amount of china needed to serve sizable crowds; a larder, just off the kitchen, would be filled to the rafters with meats, vegetables, and spices.

World War I brought an end to the days of plentiful resources. With food rationing a directive, gone were the extensive larders of surplus foodstores, and a well thought-out *Basic Pantry* was necessary. Not only was the supply of foods diminished — requiring ingenuity to produce a balanced meal — but certain imported seasonings were impossible to acquire, creating the need for new ideas on how to produce tasteful meals with foodstuffs that were available.

The influx of women in industry, due to the absence of fighting men, brought about the need for gadgets and kitchen conveniences to assist homemakers with less home time. Such innovations included efficient cabinetry for capsulized kitchens.

The domestic refrigerator, even in its infancy, was a welcome change from the "ice box." This was an insulated wooden box with one compartment for storing perishable food and another for holding large blocks of ice, which were delivered daily. In 1925 the first truly effective refrigerators were produced; they allowed the cook to extend the life of perishables, when available. Still, the need was quite evident for a pantry or larder, with a stock of various preserved and tinned foods to carry the family through shortages during the months when seasonal produce was unavailable.

The resourceful cooks of the World War I era stored their valued seasonings and flavoring ingredients in herb boxes. They would often grow their own fresh herbs, dry them and place them in the sectioned compartments of a small, drawered cabinet. The more affluent were able to procure dried herbs and spices in individual, small metal containers with attractively imprinted lids and covers. Sugar was available in cones, which often stood three feet tall, weighing as much as fourteen pounds. The desired amount would be cut off in chunks with sugar nippers. A room that was free of moisture and environmental influences was necessary, if not crucial, to the preservation of these sugar cones and dried herbs; thus there was a need for a dry pantry.

The needs met by a system for food storage have changed through the years as our country has grown and expanded, in times of excess and times of want. The 20th century has seen more changes in the kitchen than in all time previously, but the basic needs of cooks today remain the same as those of our earliest ances-tors. The difference lies in our more complicated — yet *comparably* effortless — way of meeting those needs. We do have to utilize our time in the kitchen more efficiently, since more time is spent out of the home by almost everyone in the family — compared to the men and women who were on the homestead the whole day. Let us be grateful to the early pioneers as we use their discoveries in our contemporary pantries and larders.

# Chapter 2

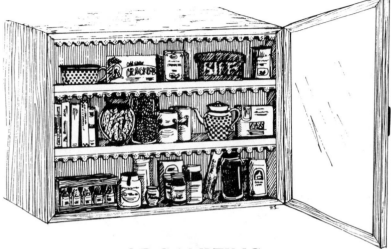

# ORGANIZING
# YOUR PANTRY SPACE

As YOU ORGANIZE YOUR PANTRY SPACE, you
need to address the pantry location. There is a method
for determining the best location for foods to be stored;
keep in mind the need to prevent spoilage and
deterioration, as well as how to save steps and time in
food preparation. In order to take advantage of the best
arrangement and storage of foods, you must determine what cupboard and areas in the kitchen utilize
and enhance your efforts.

The initial step in determining an efficient pantry
system is to analyze your kitchen floor plan, as well as
your particular cooking habits. Take out a large sheet
of paper and draw out your own kitchen floor plan:

| | |
|---|---|
| Counterspace | Sink |
| Cooktop and Oven | Cupboard Space |
| Refrigerator | Dining Areas |

7

See Diagram A for an example to follow in creating your floor plan.

DIAGRAM A

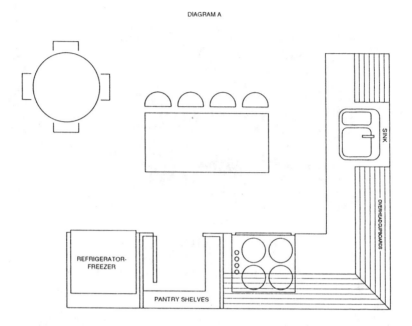

REFRIGERATOR-FREEZER

PANTRY SHELVES

SINK

OVERHEAD CUPBOARDS

After your floor plan is drawn up, consider each of the following questions, then draw the answers (using different colored pencils for each step) so that you will have a guide to use in reorganizing your pantry system.

1. At which countertop or work space do I spend most of my time in food preparation? (Mark a #1 over that place.)

2. Where are my herbs, spices, and staples placed? (Mark a #2 over that location.)

3. What steps do I make in the kitchen as I am preparing meals? Draw *dotted* lines to indicate your movements about your kitchen. (Mark a #3 between the dotted lines.) Now, comparing your

own diagram to Diagram B below, make sure that you have all the markings before moving to question #4.

DIAGRAM B

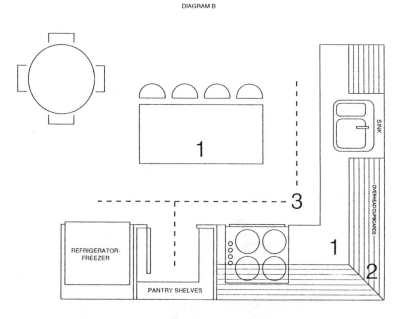

4. Does my culinary lifestyle lend itself to using prepared foods such as canned or packaged, or do I utilize fresh foods as often as possible? Mark a #4 on your refrigerator, if you use mostly fresh: mark a #4 on your pantry cupboards and freezer, if prepared goods are your choice. For readers who use both about equally, there will be a #4 on both locations.

Now it is necessary for you to understand your *work triangle*. This is the pattern developed by kitchen designers for strategically placing fixtures and appliances to save steps in the kitchen. With your numbering complete, now draw three *solid* lines, with a different colored pen or pencil. Connect one solid line from refrigerator to sink, one line from sink to cooktop or stove, and one from stove to refrigerator. See Diagram C.

DIAGRAM C

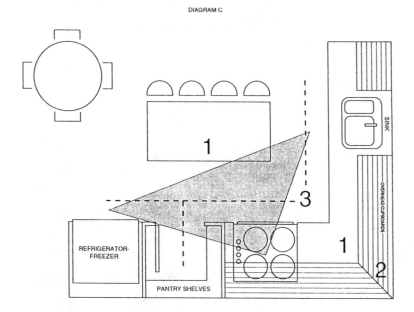

An optimum triangle is a workspace which requires the user to move a minimum of 12 feet, but no further than 22 feet, in a triangle pattern defined by location of refrigerator, sink and cooktop. When a kitchen triangle is below or beyond these standards, kitchen habits are affected. Either you will be required to adjust your storage capacities to suit a smaller (but still efficient) pantry, or you will realize that you need extra time to get the job of food preparation done in a kitchen that has you retracing steps in order to reach necessary items or work areas. This brings us back to the first question:

## *At which countertop or work space do I spend most of my time in food preparation?*

Is your food preparation area — where you have marked #1 — located on the counterspace between your sink and stove? Or, if not situated precisely between your sink and stove, is your food preparation area at least within the parameters of the work triangle (solid lines)? For example, on Diagram C, the food preparation area could easily be on the island, yet still be close to the cabinets where this cook keeps often-used food items (space #2).

One way to alleviate the problem of a dislocated food preparation area is to rearrange your cabinets so that often-needed foods (such as spices or staples) are placed over your food preparation area #1. An alternate plan is to assemble your ingredients — especially the needed seasonings — before preparing your foods. For example, try using two or three small dishes, especially if the recipe is complicated or if there are many different preparation stages to the recipe you are following. Measure out and blend ingredients appropriately, combining seasonings in the same dish if they are to be added to the recipe at the same stage. This not only saves time by enabling you to cook efficiently, but it is also visually motivating. Such techniques can give you a sense of pride, for you are appropriating the very skills that professional chefs use in creating their culinary masterpieces. We now move to question #2:

## *Where are your herbs, spices, and staples placed?*

Do you have and use a spice rack — which you probably received as a wedding present — hanging on the wall above your stove? Or do you have your staples and seasonings in the cupboard next to or above your cooktop? One of our biggest problems is not fully understanding the use of herbs and spices. The *shelf life* of seasonings — as well as that of certain staples — is equally important. Refer to the "Resource Guide" for specifics on these items.

For now, on your diagram, look at your cupboard areas or pantry to ascertain whether you store your most used items such as spices, staples, and condiments within reach of your food preparation worktop. If not, you may be expending needless steps moving about in your kitchen during food preparation.

Many stories have been told of people who used to keep a spice rack — with clear, attractively filled bottles all in a row — on the wall above their cooktop until the ground seasonings inside became so hard they couldn't prod them loose, even with an ice pick! They presumed that the seasonings were hard because of age, but they had probably become glued together by natural humidification. Each time a jar was opened near or over the pot in which food was already cooking, steam would sneak inside the jar. The steam then become trapped by those wonderful plastic bottomed stoppers which came with the bottles. Another common *faux pas* is committed when the spice cupboard is left open while we cook. We do this so that we can see what we need as the recipe develops, reaching for it at the appropriate time. However, nothing spoils the life and flavor of herbs and spices quicker than light and moisture (hydration).

Thus we see that those clear bottles of herbs and spices — even if the jars are opened away from the pot — can present a problem. Neither should we store them in a cabinet which is opened so often that light and moisture will pour in. The dilemma lies in two requirements: we want the seasonings positioned to save steps and maximize efficiency, yet we need to find a location which provides a dry, dark place. When we handle the spices and herbs, we want to avoid the damaging effects of environmental conditions which kitchens, by their nature, present.

Storing herbs and spices in a cupboard that maintains a dark, dry atmosphere is most ideal. An ideal location is a tiered spice drawer, which makes it possible to avoid rummaging through cupboards full of little jars and tins. Most herbs and spices should be used within a year; date the tins or bottles when you purchase them. Unfortunately, the flavor value of herbs and spices can be lost within two months if they aren't stored properly. Another suggestion is to alphabetize your seasonings while you are organizing your cupboards; this will alleviate the typical shuffling around in the cupboards.

When a spice or herb is needed for seasoning a dish, open the spice cupboard or drawer once, get out the necessary items and close the door/drawer. When measuring the ingredients, keep them away from heat and moisture. After the seasonings have been measured into a dish, the containers should be put away promptly. These steps will extend the shelf life and pungency of your seasonings and improve the flavor of all the dishes you prepare.

Flour and sugar can be kept in resealable glass jars or plastic containers; light doesn't affect these staples as much as moisture can.

As you are rethinking the positioning of the most used cupboards in your kitchen and pantry, think now about the third question:

### What steps do I make in the kitchen as I am preparing meals?

Many cooks have their foods and preparation areas scattered around the kitchen in a haphazard way. Although some like it that way, others prefer to organize.

Do you constantly have to crisscross the kitchen or kitchen island to reach often-used items? Check your diagram's dotted lines, then consider switching cupboard usage to alleviate this problem. For example: move your seasonings and staples to the cupboard over the food preparation area, then put your everyday serving ware (dishes, trays, flatware) in the cupboards and drawers near the cooktop. With this maneuver, your seasonings and staples are in a safer environment and you have created an efficient means for serving up meals right from the stove. In addition, you have cleared cupboard space over and near your food preparation area, enabling you to utilize the cupboards available there more easily.

With the kitchen and pantry cupboards organized, now think about *how* and *what* you cook. This is where the fourth question comes in:

**Does my culinary lifestyle lend itself to using prepared foods such as canned or packaged, or do I utilize fresh foods as often as possible?**

This question presents the need to introduce the term *Perishables Pantry*: a place to store the foods and seasonings — such as fresh herbs and assorted cheeses — which require a controlled, cool environment to maintain their food value, yet are needed close at hand during the cooking process. Your refrigerator!

If your cooking needs are met by dry goods and packaged foods, your *Perishables Pantry* will be smaller than if you used fresh foods more often. If this is your style, you will want to arrange all of your packaged foods within reach of your food preparation area, enabling you to enjoy the swift food preparation which packaged foods allow.

One of the most important things to learn about storing food items is that many staples and seasonings require refrigeration — or even freezing — for optimum shelf life and less waste. When you properly utilize the available space in your refrigerator and freezer to store foods, staples, and seasonings, your cooking potential is unlimited. For example, shelf space taken up by canned or granulated chicken stock is cleared for other use by keeping homemade stock in your freezer.* The flavor difference is immense, and utilizing the parts of meats, poultry, seafood and vegetables which you

*See Chapter 4, "The Freezer Pantry," for more information.

might usually throw away is economically, environmentally and nutritionally wise.

Here's something else to consider when you think of freshness and flavor: do you make a habit of using fresh parsley instead of dried? What a difference to the resulting dish it makes, compared to dried. However, you cannot store fresh parsley on the pantry shelf and expect it to stay moist and bright green. Try standing fresh parsley in a jar of water and place it in the refrigerator; keep a plastic bag over the top of the jar to maintain the necessary cool humidity. (Fresh parsley is a great source of vitamin C.)

The refrigerator/freezer appliance plays an integral part in the *triangle* of your working kitchen. As you learn more about staples and seasonings — as well as foods themselves — you will become increasingly aware of the need for a designated area in your refrigerator for a *Perishables Pantry*. The main rule to remember is that cooked and uncooked foods should be kept separated.

To some people, having a *pantry* may indicate an elaborate room with climate controls, wine racks filled to the brim with vintage bottles for long term aging, and an unlimited array of backup food items to bring out when necessary. The truth of the matter, however, is that most of us have mini-pantries located in cupboards around our kitchens and larder contents spread out in available storage areas around our house and garage. There is nothing wrong with this arrangement, as long as you aren't making more work for yourself by having to take too many steps to retrieve a particular item. A pantry is actually more *what* you store than *where* you store.

A pantry can be anywhere, as long as it is free from excessive heat and moisture, and bright light is limited; the ideal is for the room or cupboard to be completely dark. If you have an older home which has a broom cupboard in the kitchen, utilize this for your pantry. If your area of storage is a few shelves in the garage (north wall is coolest), so be it. Many of you may have pantries for storage right next to the kitchen, or you may use your utility room; no matter where your primary pantry is, you still need a pantry cupboard *in* your kitchen to hold the items for which you constantly reach during the day. Any system which works *for* you instead of *against* you is terrific.

Your kitchen should reflect the sequence of events which you go through in the cooking process. Store utensils used for preparing foods in the drawer under your food preparation area; the utensils used during the cooking process should be placed near the cooktop. (This sounds obvious, but it's easy to overlook simple ideas when caught up in complicated ones.) Try a wall mounted magnet bar above your stove to keep most-used utensils and knives within quick grasp, or hang them from a rack above the cooktop. This alleviates such frustrating activities as digging through the scores of measuring cups for a metal spatula. With this system, you will have less clutter and can quickly grab the utensil needed at your cooktop. (You'll find that this effort may eliminate *the junk drawer.*)

After thinking through your kitchen habits, analyzing your floor plan, and acting on the layouts you chose, you will begin to reap the rewards of having a more organized kitchen and efficient pantry space. Now for the next challenge: learning what is needed to fill these spaces, so that the pantry will begin to work for you.

# Chapter 3

# A BASIC PANTRY:
# WHAT MOTHER HUBBARD
# NEVER KNEW

THE EMPTY CUPBOARD — NOT EVEN A BONE...
How many times have we felt just as old Mother Hubbard did, when taking an inventory of available foodstuffs in our cupboards? It isn't for lack of trying. Everyone grocery shops. Maybe that's our problem; we haven't known what to shop for. As you glance over the following basic pantry menu, you may find your head swirling due to the scope of it; but have no fear! There is a way of going about this that is easy and inexpensive, and you will find that many of the listed items already have a place in your existing cupboards.

## *BASIC PANTRY MENU*

**Miscellaneous Grains:**

*Hard flours* — unbleached white, all-purpose, whole wheat, self-rising (for varieties of cooking and baking needs)

*Specialty flours* — cake flour, pastry flour or whole wheat pastry flour

*Cereal grains* — oats (regular and instant), yellow cornmeal, wheat germ, bran, grits, farina, wheat flakes, preferred hot cereals (necessary fiber for our balanced diets)

**Prepared Mixes:** biscuit mix (or BISQUICK), pancake mix, cornbread mix (They make quick breads a breeze.)

**Rices:** long grain white rice, instant (or converted) rice, brown rice*

**Pasta:** spaghetti, linguini, wide egg noodles, fettucini, lasagna, ravioli, macaroni, tortellini, spinach noodle varieties (entrée in 10 to 20 minutes)

**Starches and Thickening Agents:** cornstarch, tapioca starch (or flour), unflavored gelatins (gravy and sauce essentials)

**Sweetening Agents:** granulated sugar, superfine sugar, confectioner's sugar, light and dark brown sugar, honey, molasses, light and dark corn syrup, pancake syrup, liquid or powdered artificial sweeteners (if desired) (See also Chapter 6, "The Dessert Pantry.")

**Oils and Fats:** olive oil (virgin and extra virgin), corn oil, salad oils (vegetable or safflower), peanut oil, vegetable oil spray, lard, shortening, margarine or butter — 1 stick at room temperature, 1 pound in *Perishables Pantry*

*Keep a supply of already made rice in the freezer.
See Chapter 4, "The Freezer Pantry."

Vinegars: white distilled vinegar, cider vinegar, red wine vinegar, rice vinegar

Dried Herbs: basil, bay leaves, celery seed, chives, dill weed, marjoram, oregano, parsley flakes, rosemary, sage, savory, thyme

Spices: allspice, cardamom, cayenne, chili powder, cinnamon (ground and sticks), cloves (whole and ground), curry, ginger (ground), mace, dry mustard, nutmeg (whole nut and grated), paprika, pepper (ground and whole), white pepper, lemon pepper

Seasonings and Condiments: granulated salt, coarse salt, seasoning salt, garlic salt, garlic powder, ACCENT flavor enhancer (msg), mayonnaise, tartar sauce, ketchup, yellow mustard, Dijon mustard, assorted salad dressings, soy sauce, hot sauce, chili sauce, teriyaki sauce, barbecue sauce, Worcestershire sauce, horseradish, pickles (sweet and dill), assorted pickle relishes, packaged gravy and sauce mixes (such as brown, chicken, *au jus*, hollandaise, taco and enchilada)

## Essentials For Preparing Foods:

Beef, chicken, vegetable stock (powdered or canned); also fish stock (or clam juice), tomato paste, tomato sauce, tomato juice, vegetable juice, canned enchilada sauce, marinara (assorted types), cranberry sauce (gel and whole berry), green chilies, dried onion flakes, bacon bits, fresh bread, poultry stuffing, croutons, fine bread crumbs, prepared soups (dried onion, tomato, cream of: mushroom, celery, chicken, cheddar cheese, and potato), meat tenderizer, popcorn

## Essentials For Preparing Breads And Basic Desserts:

Active dry yeast (cake or powder), baking powder, baking soda, cream of tartar, sweetened condensed milk, evaporated milk, nonfat dry milk, coffee granules, chocolate squares (bitter, semi-sweet, white), cocoa powder, chocolate chips, peanut butter, jams or jellies, coconut (flaked), food coloring, extracts (almond, cherry, chocolate, lemon, maple, mint, orange, rum, vanilla) See Chapter 6, "The Dessert Pantry," and Chapter 9, "A Larder of Extracts, Liqueurs, and Spirits," for an expanded menu.

### Essential Canned Goods:

*Meats, Fish, and Seafood* — canned chicken, turkey, ham, corned beef hash, tuna, crab, shrimp, clams, sardines (This supply will save you on those emergency days.)

*Vegetables* — corn (creamed and kernel), carrots, peas, leaf spinach, green beans, potatoes, yams, beets, mushrooms, tomatoes (stewed and whole, unsalted), pimentos (sliced or whole), green stuffed olives, black pitted olives, sauerkraut

*Fruits* — peaches, pears, pineapple (sliced and small chunk), fruit cocktail, mandarin oranges, cherries, assorted pie fillings (*e.g.*, apple, cherry, peach), dried fruits (*e.g.*, apricots, prunes, raisins)

*Nuts* — peanuts, almonds (whole, sliced, slivered), cashews, walnuts, pecans, sunflower seeds (great source of dietary fiber)

### Canned and Dried Legumes:

Navy beans, pinto beans, kidney beans, garbanzo beans, lentils, split green peas (Make a quick bean salad by combining chilled leftover beans with Italian dressing.)

### Perishables and Fresh Produce:

(Store in refrigerator unless otherwise noted.)

*Dairy Products* — cheeses (cheddar, jack, Swiss, cream, cottage, ricotta, Parmesan or Romano), milk, cream, sour cream, butter, margarine, eggs

*Meats and Fish* — Having a proportional amount of ground beef, ground pork, and white fish fillets available in your *Perishables Pantry* each week will provide a basis from which to create meals if you do not wish to plan meals ahead. Purchase preferred cuts as needed or desired. Generally, store meats and fish in the refrigerator for no more than two days prior to cooking; keep in the freezer for maximum storage benefits. (See "Resource Guide" for specifics.)

*Vegetables* — carrots, celery, salad greens, tomatoes, yellow onions, green onions, garlic, potatoes, other vegetables to your preference (*e.g.*, broccoli, cauliflower, spinach), parsley. (Note: yellow onions need dry, circulating air; place them in a netted bag or wire basket and store on a dry pantry shelf. Brown winter potatoes should be stored in the dry pantry, too, in a brown paper bag with holes punched in it for release of gases emitted from stored potatoes.)

*Fruits* — apples, bananas (store in dry pantry until ripe, then refrigerate), grapes, oranges, grapefruit, lemons and/or limes

## Wines and Spirits for Cooking:

Dry white wine (dry vermouth is a good substitute; never buy "cooking wine"), dry red wine, Marsala, dry and sweet sherry, rum, assorted liqueurs (See Chapter 9, "Larder of Extracts, Liqueurs, and Spirits," for more complete information.)

## Beverages:

Milk, fruit juice, soda pop, mineral water, club soda, tonic water, purified water, coffee, tea

\* \* \*

Now that a complete pantry has been described, there are some specific points to be made concerning implementation.

First, this is, virtually, a *complete* pantry. If you decide that some of these items would not be used in your kitchen, don't stock them. An item which is not used takes up valuable space on your pantry shelf. You may find, however, that having items on hand which you do not normally use allows you to expand your recipes and use substitutions more effectively.

Second, this is a dry pantry *and* perishables pantry menu. Some items must be stored in your refrigerator. (See "Resource Guide" for any item about which you are unsure.) If you take an inventory of your cupboards and refrigerator after reading this menu, you will probably find many of the items listed for a *Basic Pantry*. Completing your *Basic Pantry*, therefore, can be achieved during three or four regular shopping trips; then you can move on to stocking your *Freezer Pantry*.

Third, when you are ready to begin stocking your shelves, think of your pantry as you would think of your home when preparing to redecorate. Decorating takes imagination as well as time. You cannot and should not rush out to complete your pantry in one afternoon. When you make out your next shopping list, place on the list a few of the items which you would like to add to your pantry — starting with those of greatest importance to your particular culinary style. As you do this each shopping trip, think about ways in which this particular purchase might help or enhance your cooking habits; either make a mental note of it as you add it to your pantry or maintain a card file with notes on your pantry inventory. (See CARD BOX in "Resource Guide.")

Finally, with your choice items stocked, try a few of the other items which you find interesting. Before purchasing, look up the item in the "Resource Guide" to see its uses, storage needs, and any other helpful hints. You will find this guide an invaluable source of new ideas, even for those items which you have already stocked or with which you are familiar.

Also, familiarize yourself with the other pantry menus included in this book. You'll then have a better understanding of pantries and larders, not only as they relate to specific needs — as the *Dessert Pantry* does — but also as they pertain to diverse culinary needs — as the *Gourmet Larder* does.

Even the greatest chefs need inspiration to keep abreast of changes in their competitive field. All of us can profit from the ideas of other culinary lifestyles, even if we don't take on that particular bent ourselves. *All* of us need tools in this hectic society to keep our home life as peaceful and nurturing as possible. This concept is one of those tools; the genesis of great cooking, your *Basic Pantry*.

# Chapter 4

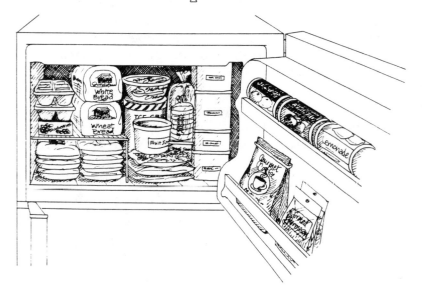

# THE FREEZER PANTRY

Y OUR *BASIC PANTRY* SYSTEM, consisting of both *Dry Pantry* and *Perishables Pantry*, can be refined with the addition of the *Freezer Pantry*. There is nothing more efficient in terms of saving time in cooking — as well as in preserving foods — than the freezer. The refrigerator is affected by variables such as temperature and environmental influences (especially if you have teenagers making a revolving door of your refrigerator door); therefore it is not the most ideal place for long term food storage. The freezer, however, has a steady, controlled environment — at or below 0° Fahrenheit — which is of utmost importance in maintaining the best quality of food and retaining the original flavor. Another important aspect of the *Freezer Pantry* is the freedom it gives for preparing meals ahead and keeping special embellishments readily available.

Now that you are familiar with the basic pantry menu, you will notice the repetition of some of the items, including foods and staples which can be incorporated into time saving habits for your cooking needs. This occurs because some basic items needed in our kitchens can be stored longer and more efficiently (especially if purchased in large quantities) in the *Freezer Pantry*.

The basic rules in freezing are: 1) seal tightly, after removing as much air as possible from around the foods you wish to freeze; 2) cool all hot or warm foods before placing them in your freezer, or you will raise the temperature in the compartment, possibly causing spoilage of other foods contained there; 3) label and date all foods placed there. Don't trust your memory; it goes on vacation when you need it most!

## FREEZER PANTRY MENU

(See "Resource Guide" for frozen food duration.)

### *Freezer Essentials:*

*Homemade Stock and Liquids* — beef, chicken, vegetable, and seafood stock. Keep small containers in your freezer in which to drain off juices from canned foods and liquids used in preparing foods. For example, to add flavor when making chowders, stir in seafood liquids from such items as canned salmon, tuna, shrimp and clams — which you have reserved and saved in the freezer. Do the same for canned vegetable liquids and liquids used to steam, sauté or boil vegetables; the reserved liquids stored in your freezer are handy for making vegetable stock, soups, gravy and sauces. Also reserve canned fruit liquids for adding to juices or desserts instead of water. Three sixteen-ounce containers should do: one for reserved seafood liquids, one for vegetable liquids, and the other for reserved fruit juice liquids. (You can also freeze any liquids used in preparing poultry or beef for future stock making. (See "Resource Guide.")

*Specialty Grains and Flours* — semolina flour, whole grain flours, wheat berries

*Meats* — roasts, preferred cuts of beef, veal, chicken, turkey, lamb, pork, various sausages, bacon, salt pork, assorted ground meats

*Fish and Seafoods* — such items as preferred fish filets, shrimp, lobster and clams, as needed for prepared meals

## *Freezer Indispensables:*

*Frozen Vegetables* — spinach, peas, corn, artichoke hearts, baby corn, mushrooms, and other such items

*Frozen Fruits* — strawberries, raspberries, blueberries, blackberries, fresh local berries

*Breads and Pastries* — french bread, sandwich loaf, bread dough, pizza dough, pie dough, biscuit dough, puff pastry, phyllo dough, assorted cookie doughs, bread crumbs, crepes, corn and flour tortillas (This is a wonderful way to save money: buy bread products when they are on sale and freeze them.)

## *Dairy Staples:*

Ice cream, whipped cream, milk, whole and grated cheeses (Parmesan or Romano, Swiss, cheddar), unsalted and salted butter, margarine, soft cheeses (cottage and ricotta) (See "Resource Guide" for information on changes in texture for cheeses after freezing.)

## *Miscellaneous Items:*

Coffee beans, ground coffee, fruit purees, vegetable purees, parsley tops, pesto, 1 to 2 cup portions of cooked white rice, crumb toppings

*Prepared Alternate Meals* — these can be leftovers or a dish from a double batch from preparation day

You will develop your own system of using your *Freezer Pantry*; each of our lifestyles has different needs. For example, one cook started with learning how to plan for leftovers, since they were a common occurrence in her home; the benefits were immediately visible. Instead of planning to serve the inevitable leftovers the next day, she would — immediately after serving the first portions — place the extra food in a new dish, freeze it and serve it the next week with different accompaniments. The satisfaction this can give is an incredible motivator. Not only can you be free from cooking on another day, but everyone will think the meal was freshly assembled. Of course you must choose meals which freeze well; avoid all dishes with fresh potatoes, for they lose their texture and can become mush-water when thawed.

Another plan which may suit your lifestyle is the adoption of the concept of a preparation day — one chosen day per week to spend preparing such items as stocks, desserts, and frozen dinners. You may decide — based on your schedule and available free days — that once or twice per month is best for you. Use your *Freezer Pantry* to enhance all of your gastronomical needs. You will have on hand, for example, fresh stocks for soups, stews, and sauces; assorted cookie dough for a quick-fix dessert; at least one alternate meal, such as a quiche or meat dish to which you will add a fresh vegetable on the appointed day of use; and a variety of fresh frozen ingredients to use when your patience has thinned to a sliver and laboring over the stove is the last thing for which you have tolerance.

Determine what aspects and items from the *Freezer Pantry* you would find helpful — as well as appetizing — by keeping a mental note (or a physical one, in a card file under "Freezer Menus"). For added information relating to freezer duration, steps to take when defrosting, and new ways to cook and embellish, look in "Resource Guide."

First purchase the selections which you want to acquire immediately. After stocking *your* necessary items and choices, try purchasing or preparing one or two items listed for storage in your freezer and watch how they work for you. See "Resource Guide" for specific information relating to storage times and uses of *Freezer Pantry* foods.

# Chapter 5

## SHOPPING FOR YOUR PANTRY

ONCE YOU ARE FAMILIAR WITH THE *Basic Pantry* and the *Freezer Pantry* menus, a systematic approach to filling your shelves is helpful. While shopping to complete your pantry may seem an arduous task, it can be fun and interesting if you take it in small steps. Now that you can visualize how your culinary style is going to be enhanced by having a well stocked pantry, you need to set some priorities.

The **first step** is to complete your *Basic Pantry*. Begin a perpetual shopping list which can hang on your refrigerator or kitchen bulletin board; this list is for *any* item which you realize you need as your week progresses. Be it a pad of paper or a roll of adding machine tape — which you can revolve as you use it — *always* keep a running tally of the things you need. Each time you shop, add an item or two which you need for stocking your *Basic Pantry*. You'll be amazed

29

at how quick and inexpensive it is to actually complete your pantry. In addition, you'll experience a peace of mind, knowing that you don't have any pending culinary shortfalls.

Once your *Basic Pantry* is complete, the second step is to analyze your own style of cooking and eating. For example, do you lean toward the more complicated foods? If so, turn to "The Gourmet Larder." You'll find listed there the items which will enable you to successfully turn out the most intricate recipes. To lessen the expense in completing your *Gourmet Larder*, purchase one or two items each time you shop, or buy them when they are on sale. On the other hand, if "little people" and/or a spousal equivalent are part of your life at this time, you may choose to take a look at the *Family Larder* for those items which can make meals for your family an easier task. This larder will also give you ideas which can encourage you when you are at the end of your imaginative wits.

For those of us who have certain dietary needs — such as low cholesterol diets or vegetarian pursuits — your pantry will be a combination of specific items from *all* of the pantry categories. In the pantry menus, you will find items referring to your own special needs, as well as those which you may want to delete. It is still beneficial, however, to have the *Basic Pantry* complete, since our social lives are comprised of people with varied tastes and culinary philosophies.

The third step is to keep a note of *Basic Pantry* items which your household exhausts quickly; store larger quantities of those products. This has a two-fold purpose: you won't run out of a much-used item as frequently, and you can save money purchasing in large amounts (providing you use the food before spoilage). Try using a few of the substitution ideas from the "Resource Guide," and experience a variety of tastes and textures to make the foods you often cook more enticing. As you learn more about seasonings and staples and the ways in which they affect and change our foods, you will find yourself expressing your creativity with foods for which you had previously dreaded following a recipe.

With shopping list in hand, make your purchases at the supermarket wisely. The important things to remember as you shop are these:

- Check perishable foods for expiration dates.

- Notice whether poultry and seafood are truly fresh or were frozen — and thawed. Freezing affects storage and shortens cooking time.

- Question whether a particular purchase is something which will provide nutrition and save time or money, or whether it is just a fad product.

- Be aware of labels. Consider cost per unit, either lb/mg or oz/gm. Look for nutrition information, grade of quality on canned goods (A-C), and product dating. Cultivate your consumer awareness and comparison shopping skills, in order to make the most knowledgeable purchases.

- Shop with a calculator to tally your purchases, and make budget alterations if needed.

- Try to purchase as many foods, seasonings, and staples as you can without manufacturer's packaging, such as boxed cereals. You pay a lot for packaging, which is not only another form of advertising, but a source of waste for our landfills — unless it is recyclable. New laws are presently being enacted to improve the standards by which grocers maintain their bulk foods. You not only save money on your purchases when buying in bulk, but you also buy less packaging — the stuff of overloaded landfills, an environmental concern for us and our children.

- For optimum results, purchase spices and dried herbs in small quantities and use within one year. Label with care all herbs and spices with purchase date, and if you don't think you can go through your allspice in one year, for example, share half of it with a friend. For already-purchased seasonings, check the aroma of the herb or spice; unless it is still sharp and vivid, toss it out or try using as much as double the recipe requirement, in order to use all of it quickly. Remember to taste as you season, making a note of the quantity you used.

- When you go into the grocery store, go to the produce department first, then go on to dry goods, staples, meat, and dairy; pick up the frozen foods last. It is amazing how much junk we put into our baskets by meandering around when we shop. If you are on a food budget, this orderly shopping mentality keeps you purchasing with priorities in mind. Once you have met your shopping list, *then* you can shop for extras. See the appendix for a master shopping list.

- If you need to cut costs, try using generic brands. Often the only drawback to generic foods is that the appearance isn't as uniform, but flavor is still "acceptable." It doesn't matter whether the peaches, for example, are whole or in pieces if you are going to puree them and add them to a dish. (In cooking and baking, you will find the optimum flavor results from using the best quality products; the generic choice is in your spending priorities.)

- Shop for your favorite supermarket and make the most of your purchases there. Running around to different stores doing a coupon chase ends up costing you valued time as well as money. Most coupons are a low cost draw to

bring you in for the other high cost purchases.
Be aware of this trap!

- If you would like to learn to plan more of your
  meals ahead of time instead of thinking up
  ideas as you go down the supermarket aisle, try
  looking through your favorite cookbook or
  recipe file while making your shopping list.
  Pick three or four main dishes, vegetables, and
  desserts per week. If you shop every two weeks,
  double the number of planned meals. Next,
  check your larder or pantry to see what you
  don't have in stock for your choices, and make
  sure that you have those items on your list. This
  is instant meal planning, and it takes only a few
  additional minutes. It will give you peace of
  mind, knowing that your week's meals aren't
  going to have to be dreamed up at the end of a
  long day. You can take this one step further by
  trying to combine your cooking efforts so that
  you are preparing more than one meal at a time.

- If your budget can handle it, try to purchase the
  items needed for an alternate meal to have on
  hand. This can be a casserole, ground meat dish
  or quiche, for example. When you are in the
  kitchen making meals, you can prepare this
  alternate meal while all your pots and pans are
  already out. Freeze the "extra" meal for those
  days when you'd rather play tennis than go
  home to cook, or when you've spent the afternoon at the pediatrician's office and your child
  needs your attention.

- Check the condition of bargain produce. Learn
  to recognize quality. It isn't a bargain if it spoils
  before you use it.

- Try shopping for bread and rolls at bakery out-
  lets. They are often a better bargain then retail
  stores, and you can freeze these baked items
  successfully.

- Don't purchase a supermarket "buy" if it doesn't suit your family's style. It isn't a bargain if no one will eat it.

- Snack products are expensive compared to the food nutrition they provide; purchase with awareness.

- If your desire is to be a "Green Consumer," you'll learn to purchase foods with little or no waste involved. See Chapter 10, "An Earth Friendly Pantry."

- If you want to be a really smart shopper, make a record of all purchases (or save all receipts) for one month, at least — if not two — then compare and evaluate your costs on a regular basis. As you do so, you'll recognize what foods have been escalating in price and what changes your culinary style is taking.

- For specific purchasing guides you might need, see individually listed items in "Resource Guide."

# Chapter 6

# THE DESSERT PANTRY

WHY SHOULD WE HAVE ONE AREA in our pantry cupboards designated for dessert-related items? It saves steps in the long run by focusing your efforts, as well as preventing pungent fragrances in your *Basic Pantry* — like ground sage — from infiltrating the delicate aroma of dessert staples, such as vanilla powder. Another example: confectioner's sugar is usually packaged in porous plastic, which strong aromas *can* penetrate. In addition, separating dessert items allows more space on the *Basic Pantry* shelves, permitting you to increase your array of special food items, condiments and unique spices; you won't have to dig through numerous spices and staples to find your baking powder. With your *Dessert Pantry* assembled and ready for action, you can attack *any* dessert recipe with confidence.

## *DESSERT PANTRY MENU*

**Dessert Foundations:** all purpose flour, whole wheat flour, pastry flour, whole wheat pastry flour, cake flour, graham cracker crumbs, vanilla wafer crumbs, chocolate wafer crumbs, phyllo dough and patty shells (frozen)

**Sweetening Agents:** granulated sugar, vanilla sugar, superfine and confectioner's' sugar, artificial sweeteners, honey, molasses, corn syrup (light and dark), brown sugar (light and dark), praline powder, jams, jellies, and preserves

**Fats:** lard, shortening, salted and unsalted butter, margarine, vegetable oil, vegetable oil spray, sweet almond oil

**Thickeners and Leavening:** tapioca flour or starch, tapioca pearls (large and small), arrowroot, cornstarch, unflavored gelatin, baking powder, baking soda, active dry yeast powder, yeast cakes

**Extracts:** almond, anise (licorice), banana, black cherry, chocolate, hazelnut, lemon, maple, mint, orange, raspberry, rum, vanilla. Instead of extracts, you may choose to use appropriate liqueurs. (See Chapter 9, "A Larder of Extracts, Liqueurs and Spirits.")

**Liquids or Equivalents:** evaporated milk, sweetened condensed milk, nonfat dry milk, lemon juice, cranberry juice, orange juice, cream and/or half and half, bottled fruit purees or sauces, prune juice

**Other Flavorings:** whole vanilla beans (store in airtight jar or keep in sugar jar), orange and lemon rind (keep frozen), chocolate (baker's, chips, cocoa powder, sweet, semi-sweet and/or bitter), cinnamon sticks, butterscotch chips, peanut butter chips, cream of coconut, brandy, port, calvados, brown sweet sherry (Amoroso or

Oloroso), sauternes, Italian vermouth, rum, apple jack, triple sec, grenadine, Italian syrups

## Dessert Accompaniments:

*Dried fruits* — raisins (golden and brown), prunes, dates, apricots, apples, bananas

*Nuts* — almonds (blanched, slivered, sliced or whole), pecans, walnuts, hazelnuts or filberts

*Other* — whole coffee beans, whipping cream (fresh or frozen), almond paste, maraschino cherries, fruit pie and pastry fillings (apple, cherry, peach, pineapple), assorted canned fruit, shredded coconut, large and small marshmallows, candied fruits, holiday citron, canned pumpkin, mincemeat, candied orange rind, borage flowers-candied

Pre-made Mixes: biscuit mix, muffin mix, scone mix, corn bread mix, instant hot cocoa, instant mousse (chocolate and vanilla), instant cheese cake, cake mixes (white, chocolate, yellow and/or lemon, angel food, sponge)

*Puddings* — vanilla (instant and/or slow cooking), chocolate, lemon, coconut cream, pistachio, butterscotch

*Gelatins* — unflavored, lemon, cherry, raspberry, orange, strawberry, lime

Optional Accouterments: cupcake paper cups, food coloring, cake decorating kit or pastry bags with assortment of tips, assorted cookie cutters, tart pan, medium and large pie plates or tins, soufflé dish, two 8" and 9" cake pans, French wire whisk, bundt pan, angel food cake pan, large copper bowl, flour/sugar sifter, dessert molds, ramekins, birthday candles, matches, lace doilies, parchment paper, cheesecloth

You will probably keep some items, such as all purpose flour, in the staples cupboard of the *Basic Pantry*. After you have assembled your *Dessert Pantry*, you can decide which of these duplicated items you want to keep in stock in both pantries.

Some items may be unfamiliar. Look up the definition and usage in "Resource Guide." Do not stock your *Dessert Pantry* with any item that you are *certain* you will never use. A few dessert items *must* be stored in the refrigerator or freezer; keep uncooked items separate from leftovers and other cooked foods in the *Perishables Pantry*. (See "Resource Guide" for pertinent information.)

# Chapter 7

## A LARDER FOR
## THE GOURMET

THIS CHAPTER IS FOR THOSE OF YOU WHO LIKE TO TRY NEW, enticing recipes. It is also for gastronomes, whose love of food and the experience of cooking motivate them to pursue the finer pleasure of complex food preparation. However, you need a larger storehouse of a variety of foods and accompaniments to achieve this goal without frustrations. After your *Basic Pantry* is complete, you can fulfill virtually all your culinary needs with the *Gourmet Larder*.

### *GOURMET LARDER MENU*

Cereals and Grains:

*Flours* — gluten, durum, whole wheat pastry, rye, soy, millet, graham, semolina, microwave flour, buckwheat flour, rice flour, masa (corn) flour, garbanzo (chick pea) flour, other varieties as desired

*Miscellaneous grains* — polenta, white cornmeal, blue cornmeal, barley, bulgur, whole wheat berries (freeze), raw bran, buckwheat, assorted groats, *quinoa*

*Rices* — arborio (white or brown), basmati (white and brown), wild rice, Indian basmati, Japanese rice

*Pasta* — orzo, acini pepe, couscous, rice noodle, buckwheat noodle, cellophane noodle, angel hair, udon noodle, soba noodle, various dried noodle shapes as desired

Starches and Thickening Agents: arrowroot, potato starch, prepared roux (keep refrigerated), large and small pearl tapioca

Sugars and Sweet Flavoring Agents: vanilla sugar, vanilla beans, maple syrup, rose geranium sugar, orange flower water, rosewater, praline powder, canned cream of coconut, canned coconut milk, carob powder, Vermont maple syrup, rice syrup, sorghum, barley malt extract, maple granules, dairy whey

Oils and Fats: Duck fat (keep in freezer), salted and unsalted butter, virgin olive oil (golden), extra virgin olive oil (green), sesame oil, sweet almond oil, hot pepper oil (chile), hazelnut oil, walnut oil, avocado oil, grapeseed oil, larding strips (Store nut oils in the refrigerator — see Chapter 12, "Resource Guide."

Vinegars: champagne, malt, cabernet, sherry, rice wine, Chinese black, blueberry vinegar, raspberry vinegar, vinegar "mother"

Herb vinegars: lemon thyme, balsamic, tarragon

Herbs: sorrel, mint, savory, chervil, mace blades, celery leaves, cilantro leaves (coriander), tarragon

Spices: ground and whole cardamom, Cajun spice, quatre epices, five-spice powder, sea salt, kosher salt, rock salt, whole white peppercorns, green and pink peppercorns, lobster seasoning, pickling spice, turmeric, saffron, anise seed, tandoori spice, red pepper flakes

**Seeds and Berries:** caraway seeds, dill seed, coriander, cumin, mustard seed, juniper berries, poppy seeds, fennel seed, pickled peppercorns, sesame seeds

**Specialty Cooking and Baking Items:** matzo flour, fruit pectin, pickling lime, marzipan (almond) paste, fruit syrups, blueberries in syrup, apricot nectar, peach nectar, instant espresso, powdered buttermilk, macaroons, marmalade

**Flavoring Agents:** Kitchen Bouquet, liquid smoke, white wine Worcestershire, sesame paste, chili paste, curry paste, soybean paste, bean sauce, seafood seasoning (Old Bay), fish bouillon, fish sauce, clam juice, oyster sauce, hot pepper sauce, sriracha sauce, light soy sauce, tamari, vegetable bouillon, aromatic bitters, malt, Rose's lime juice, grenadine, triple sec, flavored mustards (orange, honey, raspberry, Creole, whole seed), pesto, olivada, butter buds, fines herbs

**Meats, Fish and Seafood:** panchetta, tongue, fois gras, chipped beef, anchovies, anchovy paste, sardines, fish balls, herring, bottled fresh oysters, smoked oysters and clams, salmon roe or caviar, canned salmon, mackerel, escargot, dried salted shrimp

**Canned or Prepared Vegetables:** assorted relishes, chutney, pimentos, water chestnuts, hearts of palm, bamboo shoots, artichoke hearts, celery hearts (marinated), dried mushrooms, white and/or green asparagus, sun dried tomatoes, cornichons, black brine-cured olives, Spanish olives

**Fruits:** grapefruit sections, loganberries, bing cherries, orange and lemon zest, maraschino cherries

**Soups and Mixes:** cream of asparagus, borscht, lobster bisque, vichyssoise, chicken gumbo, hollandaise, bearnaise sauce, peppercorn sauce, falafal mix, tabouli mix

**Nuts, Dried Fruits and Vegetables:** filberts/hazelnuts, Brazil nuts, macadamia nuts, Spanish peanuts, dry roasted peanuts, pistachios, pignolis (pine nuts), roasted canned chestnuts, muscatel (golden raisins), currants, figs, dates, tamarind, brickle, dried tart cherries, assorted dried mushrooms, dried chilies, garlic

**Miscellaneous Stored Goods:** whole chestnuts, grape leaves, hoisin sauce, plum sauce, capers (small are best), pickles (sweet and dill), chick peas, white cannellini beans, yellow peas, turtle beans (black), mung beans, adzuki beans, fermented black beans

**Perishables:**

*Cheese* — feta, chevre, Gouda, Emmentaler, Brie, myzithra, fontina, gruyere, Roquefort, pot cheese

*Other* — cream fraiche, buttermilk, tofu, fruit purees, fresh ginger, scallions, shallots, leeks, Spanish onions, snow peas, serrano peppers, lemon grass stalks, artichoke hearts, salt pork, ham hocks (regular and smoked), fresh lemon juice, court bouillon (keep frozen), English muffins, bread dough, patty (pastry) shells, phyllo dough, pizza bread, frozen lady fingers, pound cake

**Wines and Spirits:** For use in cooking, the following are suggested: dry white wine, white dessert wine, blush (rosé) wine, assorted reds, port, brandy, calvados, cognac, Armagnac, Grand Marnier, Pernod, frangelica, chambord, kirsch, Sambuca (anise), black currant liqueur, crème de menthe (green and white), crème de banana, crème de cacao (light and dark), crème de cassis, Kahlua, Irish cream, amaretto, framboise, Ouzo (licorice), blackberry, madeira, rum, Irish whiskey, bourbon, cointreau, beer. (See Chapter 9, "A Larder of Extracts, Liqueurs, and Spirits," for more information.)

Beverages: club soda, tonic water, preferred soda pop, fruit juices (such as pineapple and cranberry), vegetable juice, mulled cider and wine mix, pure water

There never will be a pleasure more enjoyable than being able to serve a fine meal to wonderful friends and family. Some enjoy the preparation as much as they delight in the praise. Planning, doing the marketing, preparing and serving a meal for these special occasions can be an imposing task. Most people see it as impossible; many see it as a challenge. There are others, however, who attempt to make the "Art of Eating" a part of everyday life.

Often we come across ideas for a delicious and wonderful meal while looking through cookbooks or seeing a program about certain foods; we may partake of an interesting meal at a restaurant or in someone's home. We are energized by fine food, so we plan an occasion around a meal or suit the meal to an already-planned event. With our recipes in hand, we spend an hour at the market to pick up all the items on our cards or lists — if, that is, we are fortunate enough to be able to purchase all of our items at one supermarket. Many times we must go to a specialty store for a gourmet food item and a specialty grocer for fresh herbs and particular produce items which are not found in generic marketplaces. We purchase many of these items in as small quantities as we can, but this comes at a premium. Sometimes we purchase more of the specialty item than we need for the recipe; in such cases, the product may become another fabulous dish we hadn't considered at the time of purchase. Such is the inventiveness of a frugal gourmet.

Cooking is very exciting to some — not in the heartpounding sense, but in the intrinsic pleasure derived from partaking of a good meal. "Food is a celebration!" Jeff Smith, the original "Frugal Gourmet," has said. The rituals of holiday meals, special occasions, and simple — but elegant — meals with a romantic partner have been performed through the ages. Food is the great peacemaker, the family communion, the tool of romance. (Unfortunately, it can also be the fuel of fire, from grade school food fights to cold silences over a plate.) Nothing short of the five basic senses can create so much emotion, as well as satisfaction. If you think back to your own past, many of your treasured memories will have occurred where food was an integral part of the occasion.

In this hectic society, one of the last personal — and certainly time consuming — events to be hurried up, is dining well. There are times when all of us grab a fast food meal. However, few of us really feel satisfied. For the most part, we simply feel stuffed, since that is basically all we are doing — often quickly filling the empty hole in our bodies with unhealthy, non-nutritive foods — leaving an empty feeling in our gastronomical souls. Isn't it interesting that when we sit down with a loved one, friend, or associate to enjoy a meal, we can languor for hours? We are not necessarily consuming food the entire time, but the meal is the foundation on which the entire event is based. The time spent with people laughing, sharing stories, and being intimate, is so short for most of us that when we really make a special effort to experience this, it does become a celebration. As we cultivate this experience in our lives, our desire will grow for a meal which in itself is a "celebration" of tastes and textures, to savor alone or to experience with our contemporaries.

Your *Gourmet Larder* will grow as you learn and discover new gastronomical complements — as well as condiments! The items listed for your *Gourmet Larder* will enable you to prepare almost any dish which complex recipes will require, as well as suggesting that certain special ingredient to use instead of the usual staple. These will make even common foods new and enticing. *Bon Appetit!*

# THE FAMILY LARDER

T HE REASON MOST OF US DREAD THE THOUGHT of family meal preparation is that the end result often belittles the effort it takes to produce it. Much cognitive thought goes into the activities related to food preparation, and most of us do this subconsciously, never giving ourselves credit for the skills we have developed. Others simply avoid the idea altogether, not having the natural or (supernatural) ability to put together all of the planning, shopping, and preparation that go into feeding their families. Those who *do* attempt and succeed at serving a nutritious, appetizing meal, often feel taken for granted when the recipients of all of that effort simply gobble it down without a thought. (Even worse is to hear a question from a typical four-year-old when seeing something new put on his plate: "What is that?")

It is certain that the phenomenon of leftovers occurred as soon as our earliest forefathers and mothers had children. It is believed that if leftovers were something that a cook had *planned* — instead of its happening as a result of unwanted extras, a finicky eater, or a spouse who had a late meeting — then leftovers wouldn't have retained such a negative connotation over the years. We can change this mindset here and now, by altering our habits to include *planovers* in our family menu planning.

Aside from planning what to cook, a family meal manager needs to put into effect the knowledge of how to store the foods purchased, in order to avoid waste as well as using skills that conserve energy and time.

The use of time-saving equipment can be a paradox, for often the machine or gadget which saves the preparation time of a certain food negates its value in the time it takes to clean it up after use. The microwave, however, is now found in 90% of American homes, and many have found that it is *one* time saving device that is necessary in a busy household! You will have to determine what other devices in your own kitchen *are* helpful and truly time saving. The "Resource Guide" in the back of this book will provide you with information about how to best invest in, store, and utilize food products and planovers to preserve the quality and avoid waste of the foods you purchase and prepare.

Below is an addendum to the *Basic Pantry* categories for meal managers who need a little cooking "magic."

## *FAMILY LARDER MENU*

Grains: As we analyze the *Basic Pantry* Menu, there is one new item relating to family needs as far as grains are concerned. Recently developed and now being tested is *microwave flour*. It can be used for many dishes, and it allows better results from baking which is done in the microwave — no more spongy cakes! Look for it on your market's shelves or in specialty shops.

You may have noticed the exclusion of cold cereals in the cereal/grain section of the *Basic Pantry* Menu. Nevertheless, they are necessary for the *Family Larder*, for two reasons: 1) When family members are pressed for time (almost all of the time), a bowl of one's favorite cold cereal with toast and juice for breakfast is better than skipping that all-important meal of the day. This is especially so for children and young adults who need their brain power energized in the morning before they go to school. 2) You can mix cold cereal or use it as a topping for old fashioned, hot oatmeal to make the porridge more enticing. It makes sense to purchase a box or two in the brand you like — to keep on hand for the most hectic mornings; try not to get yourself into the habit of *just* serving packaged cold cereal. The kids' favorite brands are usually the ones with the most sugar, not the most nutritious. There's a recipe included in the "Resource Guide" for homemade granola, which you can embellish with a few family favorites to create a pleasing and nutritious meal.

Rices: Prepare four cups of rice ahead of time and freeze in two cup portions. These can be brought out for quick casseroles on those busy days when you get home and realize that you don't have a prepared dinner in the refrigerator or freezer, and it's 7:00 and counting. You can also add cooked rice to ground meat dishes, not only to extend the resulting dish but also to add texture, flavor, and nutritive value.

Pasta: Use pasta as often as you can with meals. It's a nutritious, inexpensive meal extender (especially good for filling teenagers' tummies), and there are so many various ways to use it — with cream sauces and a little cheese, tossed with pesto and served with French bread and, of course, with marinara sauce.

Another great idea for the family is to keep alphabet pasta on hand to make a quick soup lunch when you're suddenly required to feed all of your children's neighborhood friends. Take out a can or two of beef broth (or your homemade beef stock) and bring to a boil in a medium saucepan; add water to taste and then throw in a handful or two of the alphabet pasta. When it reaches a boil again, add a handful of fresh or frozen peas and carrots, and simmer 10 minutes. This makes a hearty soup in no time at all to accompany sandwiches. The kids will love it.

**Starches and Thickening Agents:** One important item for the *Family Larder* is dried potato flakes — not just a starch, but a thickener which you'll use often. You can use the flakes to thicken cream soups and extend meat and vegetable casseroles. With the advent of children into your life, potato flakes will take on even greater meaning. When there are babies to feed, use potato flakes mixed with liquid formula to provide an alternative to those bland baby foods necessary for tender tummies. When they are toddlers, any food with texture — meaning food with chunks in it — can and will be redeposited on the spoon or plate; a quick bowl of mashed potatoes is a life saver, and you can add some dried meat or vegetable flakes, found in the baby food section, for more flavor and nutritional value. (You may find that dried baby food retains more of the taste and smell of *normal* food, than most canned baby foods.)

Use potato flakes not only as they are intended, but in various other dishes. This versatile ingredient can be used, for example, as an extender for such foods as ground meat dishes, a last minute thickener for cream soups and chowders, a "secret" filler for quiche, and the base for potato rolls. The possibilities are endless!

If you are committed to using all natural products

and, therefore, resist using dried potato flakes because they contain a few preservatives, you needn't disregard all of the hints above. Make up a large batch of whole fresh potatoes, mash and freeze them in one- to two-cup portions. Be aware, however, that fresh potatoes do not freeze very well, and the thickening power of fresh mashed does not equal dried. Try some of the potato flakes tips, and you may find that this particular item can become a necessary part of your family larder!

Sweetening Agents: (Refer also to Chapter 6, "The Dessert Pantry.") A bag of mini marshmallows is a necessary component of the *Family Larder*. Combine them with a little lowfat sour cream, drained unsweetened fruit cocktail (reserve that juice!), and a handful of chopped walnuts to produce a nutritious fruit salad for the family when there is no time to prepare an extensive dessert. (The trick is to make sure every little one eats the fruit portions of the salad, as well as the mini marshmallows.) To entice your family into welcoming healthy cereals — such as old fashioned oatmeal and cream of wheat — drop a few chocolate chips, peanut butter chips or butterscotch chips into the hot cereal as it cools; stir the cereal and melting chips as you add milk, and you'll need no added sugar. Another idea for a way to cut down on plain white sugar added to old fashioned cereals: mix 1 teaspoon of either vanilla sugar or brown sugar with 8-10 crushed graham crackers. Let your children sprinkle this mixture over cereal and peanut butter sandwiches for an added treat, and you will have cut down on sugar up to 50%.

Oils, Vinegars, Herbs, and Spices: These are listed completely in the *Basic Pantry* menu. For the *Family Larder*, however, be aware that children do not want or require heavily spiced foods. Another thing to remember when preparing foods to be frozen for later family meals is that vinegars, herbs and spices can be added during reheating, for best flavor; freezing can reduce the potency of seasonings.

**Essentials of Preparing Foods, Breads, and Desserts:** You may be surprised, when looking back at this category in the *Basic Pantry* menu, that items listed there are necessary to a *Family Larder*. Many of them are invaluable. The foremost is fresh, frozen, canned (or at least granulated) stock: chicken, beef, vegetable, fish. Having these on hand will save you *much* time and thought, as well as providing more flavorful and nutritious food. Try to get into the habit of making up your own — at least once a month — and freezing it in quantities which are equal to your family's needs; either in ice cube sizes or two-cup portions. The stocks will constitute a base for everything from cooked rice to parboiled vegetables; it will enrich soups and stews; it will ease preparation of a delicious cream sauce to be served over chicken for the family, as well as enhancing a rich beef burgundy for company! See "Resource Guide" for instructions on how to make the various stocks; soon you'll find that you are spending less and less time in the kitchen with this minimal effort.

Another necessity that is included in this category is *prepared marinara*. (See Chapter 12, "Resource Guide," for the basic recipe.) You may keep this in your freezer, frozen in two-cup portions on one of your cooking/preparation days (see "Resource Guide"). You may prefer, however, to purchase marinara sauce at the market; there are many quite tasty ones to be found. Keep a jar stored on your *Family Larder* shelf. Having this on hand allows you the luxury to forget to plan. If you get home late and find that you haven't any planovers in the refrigerator to heat up and serve quickly, that jar on the dry pantry shelf or container in the freezer can come to the rescue. As soon as the light goes on in your tired brain, you'll remember it. In twenty minutes — the time it takes to bring water to a boil, cook some pasta (something to always keep in stock), and bring the marinara to a simmer — you and your family will be sitting down to eat.

Another helpful suggestion for producing quick meals is to keep on hand a few canned soups, such as cream of chicken or cream of celery. You can combine various cream soups with such compatible leftovers as chicken, fish or beef, mixing them with a thawed portion of your fresh-frozen rice. During the 5-10 minutes it takes to heat the casserole in your microwave, you can prepare a vegetable to go with your main dish; you'll then serve a meal anyone can enjoy. Try a few of these ideas, and you will find yourself creating other time saving, nutritious and delicious meals!

We aren't forgetting the dessert portion of this category; the old standby which you will cherish for your family is pudding. It can be embellished with dried fruits and nuts and either fresh, canned, or planned-over frozen whipped cream.

Another hint: when you bake cookies, put at least a half dozen in a small plastic bag and freeze them to have on hand when you need a quick sidebar to a simple dessert like ice cream. They practically taste fresh-baked when defrosted, especially if you allow them to actually warm up in the oven or microwave; be careful not to overheat them. You can also whip up a batch of blueberry muffins in 25 minutes; see MUFFINS in "Resource Guide."

Meats, Fish, and Seafoods: Using frozen, canned and planned-over meats will allow you greater freedom from daily meal preparation than you can imagine possible, if you haven't tried it. Looking back at the *Basic Pantry*, you will see items which should be kept on hand to enable you to proceed as an efficient meal manager. For example, a delicious down-home meal — one low in cost — is beef hash made with planned-over pot roast or rump roast cut into cubes, mixed with fresh or frozen hash browns or baked potatoes (cubed), chopped onions, and fresh gravy or a package of brown gravy mix. You can prepare a quick batch of fresh biscuits to accompany it in the time it takes to cook together all of the ingredients, and you'll have a nutritious, hearty meal utilizing foods you have readily available.

Many of us have gotten so used to eating from packages that we have lost the idea of what home cooking means. The fact that we use a few packaged foods doesn't mean that our cooking isn't downright home-style. We must discern for ourselves and our families the quality of culinary lifestyle with which we are comfortable, then pursue that end with whatever means are available to us. In our family, we value time as much as substance. For example, it may take a little longer to carve off all the meat left on a turkey carcass, then reserve and make stock with the bones for a mouthwatering cream of turkey noodle soup. If I don't have a lot of time, I just wrap that naked bird tightly and freeze it for use on a day when I happen to be spending time in the kitchen anyway.

Another example of a time-saver previously discussed is canned soups; they are fine for those who believe that they make an adequate meal. However, homemade soup is not only heartier, it also has a heart warming pleasure to it. This attitude toward home-style cooking may begin to prevail in many aspects of the time you spend in the kitchen; but there will continue to be days when there is not a leftover turkey or chicken in any of your pantries. At such a time, using canned soup or stock with canned turkey or chicken on hand, you can make a satisfactory facsimile of the "from scratch" version of soup and still achieve that feeling about your meal which you have when you start from scratch.

Keeping a can of crab meat around (to add to cream cheese and onion) enables you to have a quick, interesting, and tasty spread for crackers for drop-in guests. Parents often cease eating delicate or sophisticated foods because they don't have the desire to spend the extra time and money — above and beyond regular meal preparation for the simple palates of their children — to treat themselves with adult food. However it is important as meal managers in the home to recognize that we mustn't become so entrenched by the demands of family food preparation that we forget to have a special dish once in a while, for ourselves.

A can of shrimp or any fresh frozen seafood can be the delicious beginning of a seafood quiche — at little cost. Use your imagination and try to add a new dish to your regular routine. You may find one that is easy to prepare and has other benefits as well. It may be highly nutritional, time-saving, aesthetically pleasing and motivating. The praise and gratitude of your family will be immense, and you may find that you enjoy sitting down to your *own* meals a little more, too!

Vegetables and Fruits: For suggestions relating to this category, refer also to "Resource Guide" on how to best store and utilize the fresh produce which your family prefers. For your family's needs, try to prepare, once a week, a supply of fresh vegetables such as carrots, celery, zucchini and broccoli. Cut them into finger size portions and store, covered with water, in airtight containers in the refrigerator. These are great to quickly fill the extended hands of hungry children, and you can finish using them in pasta salads or stir fries at the end of the week.

Seasonal availability and cost often require the purchase of canned or frozen vegetables and fruit;

having some produce available in these forms is better than having none at all. You can learn ways to embellish and enhance canned products to make them more palatable and to use frozen produce to its best potential.

Important: Always save the liquid and juices from canned goods. In your freezer, try to keep two large plastic containers; drain out all vegetable juices into one and all fruit juices into the other. This includes the liquids in which fresh and frozen vegetables were simmered and the juices you don't need from frozen fruit after it has thawed. Refer to Chapter 4, "The Freezer Pantry," for more information on this aspect of using *all* of our available food and nutritional sources.

Dried Legumes: We *all* realize the value of these staples in our lives, both in nutritional as well as food values. Learn to use smoked ham hocks, which you can purchase at the meat market, and ham bones, which you might have left over, to make a stock for lentil or navy bean soup. This hearty soup can take a paramount position in your family's regular meal planning. Cooked legumes freeze well; when you make any soup or stews with legumes, you should try making planovers, freezing the extra meal portions for a quick meal or salad at a later date. Following these suggestions will allow you to make two or three evening meals with one effort.

Dried Fruit and Nuts: With the various forms of nuts available, your *Freezer Pantry* comes into play; refer to Chapter 4 for specific hints about using these items. Bananas, currants, raisins, dates, prunes, apricots, apples and pears — all are available dried. They make an excellent snack for growing children who need a quick energy boost. Kids like dried fruits because of their natural sweetness; they appeal to parents because they offer a healthy alternative to candy and other manufactured snacks. They appear to be more expensive than fresh fruits, but dehydrated fruits are actually *less* expensive, since you get more servings per pound. (You aren't paying for the water weight.) The substance and nutritional value are the same.

Perishables Pantry: Ideas for your family's refrigerator pantry are many. Although these items are specifically contained in the refrigerator, they may be frozen, depending on the freezing qualities of each individual item. Refer to "Resource Guide" for information pertaining to the proper storage of each.

All of us should have an assortment of favorite cheeses in our *Perishables Pantry*, including the cheeses we like for snacking and those we prefer to use as food embellishments. Many people are returning to the European custom of using cheese as an entrée in meals. Due to scientific evidence about the link between heart disease and cholesterol, however, we must choose our *fromage* wisely. We are fortunate to live in a country where labeling information has allowed us the ability to discern which cheeses — if we choose to enjoy them — are better choices than others. Read labels and decide how much cheese you can include in your daily food routines, then reap the benefits which your family will enjoy in eating this simple and delicious form of protein. For example, my children love cheese, so I do allow them a greater portion in their meals than I would for myself. I do, however, have to teach them about balanced eating habits. We shouldn't allow them to eat six ounces of cheese and skip the vegetables and fruits which should accompany it! Fortunately, cheese and other dairy products are a quick and energizing meal; you can rely on them when planning family meals, allowing your well stocked *Perishables Pantry* to be a crutch to lean on when the day hasn't gone particularly well.

Beverages: Kool-aid, powdered fruit drinks, miniature fruit drink containers — these are indispensable in the *Family Larder*. Children require plenty of fluids, and the more they vary, the more the children will drink. Kool-aid is, for example, appealing to youngsters when the fresh fruit juice has been depleted; you don't have to use all of the sugar called for in the recipe — especially if you add reserved or frozen juice and fruit liquids from your *Freezer Pantry*.

As you peruse the entire list of the *Basic Pantry*, with your own family needs and desires in mind, you will surely be inspired to come up with a few time-savers and culinary embellishments of your own. It's amazing how much more relaxed we can be in our family meal planning and preparation, if our *Basic Pantry* is focused and our imaginations have no limitations. A well stocked pantry is the vehicle to that end.

# Chapter 9

## A LARDER OF EXTRACTS, LIQUEURS, AND SPIRITS

THERE ARE MANY SITUATIONS IN COOKING which call us to reach into the flavoring cache and find the suitable enhancement for our recipe. A varied assortment of extracts and liqueurs on hand relieves us of the anxiety we might have tackling a new recipe. How many times have we looked over a new recipe, and seeing an ingredient like cointreau, close the cookbook promptly! Had we known that the orange extract in our cupboard would have sufficed nicely until we could purchase a mini bottle of the liqueur, we would have enjoyed that soufflé or gateau that very evening.

Below you will find listed the extracts and corresponding liqueurs available on the market today. Try substituting a liqueur for an extract named in any recipe; you may find that you prefer the resulting flavor better. Use the list in reverse if your recipe calls for a liqueur which you don't have on hand, then mark down that needed item on your perpetual shopping list so that you can purchase it on your next shopping trip and add it to your larder.

We begin with extracts already listed as *necessary* in the *Dessert Pantry*:

| Extract | Appropriate Liqueur or Brandy |
| --- | --- |
| Almond | Amaretto, Coconut Amaretto |
| Anise | anisette |
| Banana | crème de banana, banana schnapps |
| Black cherry | Kirschwasser, Kirsch, crème de cassis |
| Chocolate | crème de cocoa, Vandermint (chocolate mint), Sabra (chocolate orange) |
| Hazelnut | Frangelica |
| Licorice | Sambuca, Pernod, Ouzo, Galliano |
| Maple | (N/A) |
| Mint | green and/or white crème de menthe |
| Orange | triple sec, curacao, orange brandy, Grand Marnier, Cointreau |
| Raspberry | Framboise, Chambord |
| Rum | Use dark rum for best flavor in cooking. Keep a small stock of assorted rums; their use appears often in recipes. |
| Vanilla | Add a vanilla bean to one cup of rum or brandy in a bottle; seal and allow to age for three months. |
| Black currant | crème de cassis |

Other useful liqueurs and flavorings:

| Flavoring | Liqueur |
| --- | --- |
| Chocolate | Truffles |
| Coffee | Kahlua |
| Apple | Calvados, Berentzen |
| Blackberry | blackberry |
| Tangerine | Mandarin Napoleon |
| Strawberry | noyaux |
| Cranberry | cranberry liqueur |
| Pear | pear schnapps |
| Melon | Midori |
| Herbs and brandy | chartreuse |
| Honey | Bärenjäger |
| Butterscotch | Buttershots |
| Peach | peach schnapps |
| Peppermint | peppermint schnapps |
| Hazelnut | hazelnut schnapps |
| Raspberry | raspberry schnapps |
| Rootbeer | rootbeer schnapps |
| Tropical fruit | tropical fruit schnapps |
| Blueberry | blueberry schnapps |
| Wild berries | wild berry schnapps |
| Cinnamon | cinnamon schnapps |
| Macadamia | macadamia nut liqueur, Kahana Royale |

Often called for in recipes are these available liqueurs and brandies:

| | |
| --- | --- |
| Madeira — | port wine |
| Galliano — | Italian liqueur — fruity anise (licorice) flavor |
| Tuaca demi sec — | an orange/vanilla liqueur |
| Drambuie — | scotch liqueur |
| Aquavit — | a caraway flavored liqueur |
| Campari — | bitter berry |
| Cognac — | true French wine brandy |

There are miniature (6.8 oz, 200 ml) bottles of certain liqueurs and spirits available, so you can keep smaller amounts on hand with less expense in stocking your *Spirits Pantry*. They are:

| | |
|---|---|
| Armagnac — | dry brandy |
| Grand Marnier — | orange liqueur |
| Frangelica — | hazelnut liqueur |
| Midori — | melon liqueur |
| Peach Schnapps — | peach liqueur |
| Amaretto — | almond liqueur |
| Baileys — | Irish cream liqueur |
| Kahlua — | coffee liqueur |
| Drambuie — | scotch liqueur |

These are often used in making special desserts, so having them on hand is important. Other spirits and liqueurs previously listed are available in either fifths/liters or 1/2 fifths/375 mls.

If you are stocking your larder to include beverage mixing, you will need to complete your shelves with Angostura bitters (and/or aromatic bitters), grenadine syrup, assorted flavored syrups (such as Orgeat, vanilla), Rose's lime juice, cream of coconut, dry vermouth, and sweet vermouth. Having these on hand will enable you to mix almost any beverage properly.

# Chapter 10

# AN EARTH FRIENDLY PANTRY

Until recently, sensible shoppers and frugal chefs have battled the costs of escalating food prices with few victories. Enter the '90s and we find ourselves centered in the middle of another dilemma: our deteriorating environment.

Our society has been inundated with time saving products and work saving foods which we use to meet the needs of our hectic lifestyles. Unfortunately, we are finding that most of these products and food packages are major contributors to the tonnage of waste each household produces annually, from 1850 to 2500 pounds per year.

As we stock our pantries, we need to approach our choices with an attitude of "Green Consumerism." Catherine Dodd of *American Health Magazine* says, "A green consumer is someone who shops with the fate of the earth in mind..." We can take this idea into our homes as well, stocking, storing, and preserving our foods with an environmental conscience.

Initially, what we purchase becomes the basis for our "Green Consumerism." There has been a growing demand for "green" products — those which are recyclable, reusable, or compostible. Industry would like us to believe that they also have an environmental conscience, but they often have a different form of "green" in mind — dollars!

Many products in the market claim to be *natural* or *organic*. However, there are few label laws which specifically dictate what "descriptive" terms actually mean. Before you trust the advertisers' claims, read and inform yourself about ingredients and chemicals which are listed on the labels of products. A good source of information is the book, *The Green Consumer*, by Joel Makeoner, John Ellington and Julia Haib.

Another label buzz word of the '90s is *biodegradable*. From garbage bags to plastic milk jugs, from fast food packaging to disposable diapers, the term biodegradable is used freely. These products are but a sample of the favorite targets of environmental scientists, because the term *biodegradable* is so loosely used and so easily validated. Solid waste specialists agree with the NATURAL RESOURCE DEFENSE COUNCIL findings that a lot of stated *biodegradability* depends on factors not present in permanent landfills, such as circulating oxygen and water. Environmentalists and industry scientists have begun to speak out, demanding that advertising be *truthful*, as well as informative.

Those products which *are* biodegradable have an unfortunately negative side effect. There can be, due to premature chemical decomposition, a potential health risk to humans and animals. If the packaging on a product — say one that contains a toxic liquid or gas — begins to break down around the foodstuffs they package, there can be contamination, which can be a long term health risk. Therefore, *biodegradability* is not the solution to our solid waste crisis. Preventing waste generated by our lifestyles from getting to solid waste disposals in the *first* place is the best foot forward in the right direction.

Source reduction is being encouraged in the manufacturing industry. We can further this effort by hitting the waste producers where it hurts (profits), forcing them to pay attention to *consumers'* wants and needs. We can do this by refusing to purchase sources of unnecessary garbage (such as unrecyclable plastic) or toxic waste (such as environmentally unsafe household cleaners).

Other ways to have an Earth Friendly Pantry are:

Precycle by purchasing food items such as spices and staples in refillable packages or in bulk; then store them properly.

Recycle by separating and reserving aluminum cans, tin, plastic (when applicable), glass, paper, and cardboard for the local recycle center or your curbside disposal service.

Refuse to purchase environmentally unsafe products or products without a recyclable character.

Compost organic waste from your kitchen and yard; in so doing, you'll reduce your yearly landfill waste up to two-thirds.

Purchase phosphate-free detergents and products.

Grow your own organic produce or purchase pesticide-free produce and untreated fruit products.

Reuse containers, especially plastic bags, shopping bags and glass jars.

Avoid chlorofluorocarbons (CFC's), such as oven cleaners, air fresheners, mothballs and

drain cleaners, which have hidden toxins.
Avoid disposable *anything*.

Dispose *properly*: hazardous household wastes such
as paints, solvents, batteries and motor oil.
(Call your local Waste Management Service
for information.)

Conserve water supplies by turning off running
water during activities such as teeth
brushing, soaping, dish washing.

Prevent global warming by purchasing
environmentally safe items such as air
conditioners, refrigerators, light bulbs and
automobiles.

Investigate an environmental index of
manufacturers by writing to:
*A Guide to Hazardous Products*
*Around the Home*
901 S. National, Box 108
Springfield MO 65804

Call SEVENTH GENERATION, at 1-800-441-2538
for *Environmental Products Catalog*;

CO-OP AMERICA, at 1-202-223-1881,
for Environmental Choices;

WALNUT ACRES, at 1-800-433-2998,
for Organic Products.

# Chapter 11

# PANTRY PESTS

IF YOU'VE PUT TO USE SOME OF THE THINGS you've learned so far, your pantry cupboards are beginning to brim with culinary potential. No longer will you stand staring into the cupboard, trying to visualize the meager victuals there as a meal. We can use the "Resource Guide" to give us ideas for those days when our culinary imagination takes its leave; we'll have on hand the wherewithal to produce a lavish dinner with ease, or to create a simple snack effortlessly.

With our pantry well stocked and our cupboards no longer bare, we must broach a subject which requires a little delicacy: pantry pests. Your awareness should begin with your paying more attention to the foods and staples which you purchase and store in your dry pantry. Unfortunately, there is no amount of compulsive house cleaning that can ensure complete freedom from pantry pests. It *does* help to retain a certain cleanliness about your cupboard spaces, but if a pest has invaded a food product — often happening before you purchase the food — the only way to assure yourself of no infestation is to dispose of the questionable food item or freeze it for twenty-four hours. Freezing will stop the growth of any suspected pests and kill their eggs. Although this sounds spine tingling, aside from small moths or bugs which can get into your cupboards or foods, you need a microscope to see any pests present — if they are there at all!

The fact of the matter is that insects infiltrate 25% of what we harvest worldwide. Most of the pests are found in dried and prepared, packaged foods. The foods you need not worry about are canned and frozen, because the packaging and preserving process kills any pest that might be present there. One should be cautious however, about allowing frozen foods to sit out for long periods of time after thawing. As for canned food, it should be examined and not used if the can is bulging prior to opening.

Pantry pests can penetrate paper, cardboard and plastic with ease. However, you *can* safely assume that purchased foods are free of pests and transfer them into jars and sealed containers. Nonetheless, if pests *are* present when purchased and left on the storage shelf for long periods of time, larvae can grow, thus causing an infestation.

How do we recognize an infestation? If any food staples — either newly purchased or brought out from long term storage — have a bit of webbing present or have small moths flying around, the solution is to throw away the product or freeze it for twenty-four hours before sifting gently and resealing. If you follow the latter process, the foods will be free of pests as long as you don't allow recontamination. (This will occur only if you do not make sure that the food products are sealed tightly.)

If you ascertain that an infestation *has* occurred, clear out all your shelves. Any suspect foods should be frozen for twenty-four hours. Throw out any products having a visible infestation. Vacuum the shelves and clean with a non-phosphate household surface spray or diluted bleach. When the shelves are dry, you can replace foods for storage.

Other ways to avoid pests is to resist the impulse to buy too much food, leading to keeping it too long without using it. Cereals and grains which the family doesn't like or uses only seasonally are a real threat. Large quantities of dried fruit, nutmeats still in the shell, and food that has gotten damp are prime targets for pantry pests. Crack open all purchased shell nuts and store the nut meats in your freezer to avoid any infestations. Store in your refrigerator or freezer any specialty flours and grains which have the wheat germ intact or present. Due to the natural oils found in those products, they are a tempting harvest to pantry pests; storing these items as you would perishables will decrease the potential for rancidity of the oil.

An occasional "house cleaning" of your entire dry pantry is beneficial, not only in maintaining a pest-free pantry, but also in doing an inventory of all your pantry items. It is suggested that as often as you clean your refrigerator — or, at least as often as your freezer is cleaned — you should consider taking a sweep at your dry pantry. This will give you peace of mind with regard to the problem of pantry pests.

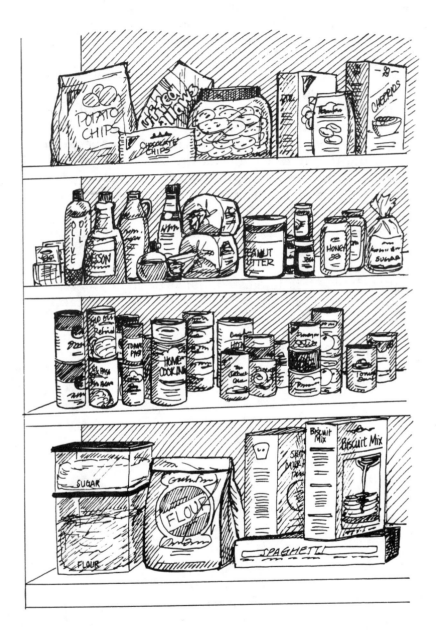

Chapter 12

# RESOURCE GUIDE

*(Fruits and vegetables mentioned for storage
will be assumed fresh unless otherwise indicated.)*

### -A-

ACCENT FLAVOR ENHANCER — This condiment brings out the flavor in foods more distinctly than salt can, because it acts on the taste buds instead of the food. It is an ingredient found in most Oriental cookery; MSG is the main ingredient.

ACIDIC LIQUIDS — These liquids are used in cooking to add flavor and create chemical reactions needed for certain food preparations. In order of acidity, from highest to lowest are: wine vinegar, cider vinegar, malt vinegar, herb vinegars, lemon juice, lime juice, orange juice, grapefruit juice, dry white and red wine.

ACINI PEPE — Pasta pellets, often called macaroni pearls, are approximately 3/8" long; when cooked, they become small, round balls.

ALLIGATOR PEAR — See AVOCADO.

ALL-PURPOSE FLOUR — Here is a blend of hard and soft wheat flours. Cooks in northern states lean toward bread baking, so all-purpose flour milled for that region would tend to be on the hard side to make better bread; meal providers in the southern states are tuned to biscuits and pies, so the all-purpose flour used there tends to be a softer blend of the two flours.

ALLSPICE — This tropical berry is used ground, as a spice. The flavor is redolent of clove, cinnamon, and nutmeg combined. It is excellent in desserts such as crème caramel or pies and is used in pickling spice.

ALMOND — See NUTS.

ALMOND EXTRACT — liquid almond flavor

ALMOND OIL — a sweet oil used in special desserts and recipes

ALMOND PASTE — Almond nut meats are ground to a fine paste to create this ingredient, which is used mainly in delicate desserts.

AMARETTO — almond flavored liqueur

AMONTADILLO — sherry, on the dry side, used for meat sauces

AMOROSO — sweet sherry, used in desserts

ANCHOVIES — This small fish is used predominantly in Greek and Italian cookery. It can be made less salty by soaking it in cool water or (preferably) milk for 10 minutes.

ANCHOVY PASTE — Made from ground anchovy meats, it is available in a tube for use in making salad dressings (such as Caesar) and many other dishes. Follow package directions for storage.

ANGEL FOOD CAKE — See CAKES.

ANISE (extract or liqueur) — liquid licorice flavor

ANISE SEED — This licorice-flavored seed is used ground in various dishes and desserts.

APPLE — Refrigerate apples for best storage. Add lemon juice when making pies, and soak in lemon water or fruit preserver before using as decorations or embellishments.

APPLE JACK — whiskey, faintly redolent of apples

APRICOT — Storage is best in the refrigerator, unwashed until used. Dried apricots can be stored in air tight containers in the dry pantry 6-12 months. (Dried apricots chop better when frozen.)

APRICOT NECTAR — a thick juice from the pressings of apricots

ARBORIO — a form of long grain rice, available white or brown, often used to make risotto

ARMAGNAC — dry French cognac

AROMATIC BITTERS — semi-bitter liquid used to flavor certain cocktails and recipes

ARROWROOT — See THICKENERS.

ARTICHOKE — Wash and refrigerate artichokes for best storage, for as long as two weeks.

ARTICHOKE HEARTS— the center, most meaty portion of the artichoke, with the pith removed; packed in light brine, marinated, or frozen

ASCORBIC ACID (Vitamin C) — This can be purchased at the drug store or in some specialty shops, in powder or tablet. It is used mainly in preserving and freezing fruits.

ASPARAGUS — Store this vegetable in the refrigerator. It will lose flavor and texture after a few days, so use it quickly. Open canned asparagus from the bottom to avoid damaging spear tips, and reserve juices in the freezer for use in stocks and sauces. When using fresh asparagus, do not discard tough ends; add them to your beef stock and simmer, then discard or simmer large ends in boiling water for 10-20 minutes and reserve liquids for later use.

ASPICS — See also GELATINS. As a general rule when making aspics, use 1 tablespoon gelatin to 1 3/4 cups liquid. The aspic mold can be lined with sweet almond oil to make removal easier.

AU JUS — This beefy tasting liquid is used for dipping beef sandwiches, and it is used in some recipes. Keep a supply of fresh, frozen, or canned beef stock to make your own au jus for French dip sandwiches. Add to 2 cups stock, 1 teaspoon or 2 cubes beef bouillon and 1/4 cup onions, sliced; simmer for 5 minutes, remove onions and serve. (You can keep an emergency supply of packaged instant au jus in your pantry, which suffices nicely when you are in a hurry.)

AVOCADOS — Store avocados at room temperature unless they are very ripe, in which case you should refrigerate them to prevent spoilage. Reserve the pit when making fresh guacamole; after it is mixed, place the pit in the dip to prevent the guacamole from browning.

### -B-

BACON — It can be kept in the freezer up to three months and in the refrigerator no longer than one week.

BACON FAT — Store it in the *Perishables Pantry* area of the refrigerator for use in sautéing some meats for added flavor, as well as for sautéing fresh greens (such as spinach) to reduce bitterness.

BAKING POWDER — This leavening agent lightens and raises the batter of baked goods. It loses its potency easily. To check the potency of your baking powder, pour 1/4 cup of hot water over 1/2 teaspoon of baking powder; if it is still fresh, it will sizzle and bubble. Homemade baking powder is easy to create; to make a teaspoon of baking powder, combine 1/4 teaspoon baking soda, 1/2 teaspoon cream of tartar, 1/4 teaspoon cornstarch.

BAKING SODA — This mildly alkaline powder is used in baking and cooking to leaven and preserve foods. At one time, we cooks were told to add baking soda to our fresh green vegetables while cooking to maintain the "green." However, we now know that this practice destroys Vitamin C.

BANANAS — Store them in a light airy room until ripe, then keep them in the refrigerator to maintain freshness. (Refrigeration will turn the skin brown, but it doesn't harm the fruit.) You can freeze banana meats; push ripe bananas through a food mill or sieve, add 1 teaspoon lemon juice or 1/4 teaspoon ascorbic acid to every 2 cups pureed bananas, place in airtight containers, label and date. Freeze this for up to 6 months and use in such foods as banana bread, cakes and muffins. For an enticing change, try slicing bananas lengthwise and sautéing them in clarified butter for a side dish or garnish for ice cream.

BASMATI — fragrant long grain rice, available white, brown (texmati) and Indian (nutty, popcorn flavor)

BASIL — This easily-grown herb is indispensable in cooking and garnishing. Try growing a kitchen herb garden near a window; when harvesting, you can wrap bunches to dry or freeze for later use. Use large leaves to wrap small crudities such as sun dried tomatoes and cream cheese or as a decorative, edible embellishment on many entrées. Mix 1/2 cup chopped basil with 1/2 cup unsalted butter and 1 tablespoon chopped shallots for a delicious butter to spread on French bread. See also HERBS.

BATTER — Try using olive oil in your batter instead of butter, for not only health reasons but for a crisper crust. Undermix pancake batter and store it in the refrigerator for as long as one week, to impede gluten development. Place plastic wrap over the surface of the batter to prevent drying.

BAY LEAVES — This is an indispensable cooking herb; the leaves are most flavorful when fresh. See BOUQUET GARNI.

BEAN SAUCE — Commonly found in red, yellow, and black bean forms, these are fermented beans with a high salt and sugar content, used as a seasoning.

BEAN THREADS — Store these in the dry pantry before use. Once cooked, refrigerate leftovers for as long as one week. They are also known as cellophane noodles.

BEANS — Either store fresh green beans in the hydrator tub of your refrigerator or blanche them in boiling water for 2-3 minutes, immerse in cold water, drain, then freeze in small freezer bags for optimum storage. Dried beans can be stored in the dry pantry eight to ten months. See also LEGUMES.

BEEF — Store it in the freezer unless it will be used within two or three days. Ground meat shelf life in the freezer is four months maximum and two or three months for best flavor; for steaks, roasts and other whole cuts, the maximum storage life is one year, 0° Fahrenheit. Use tea in water for pre-cooking tough cuts of meat; the tannin helps break down fibers. To enhance the browning of certain cuts, sprinkle caramel sugar or paprika on the surface prior to braising.

BEEF STOCK — You can brown soup bones and any other leftover beef bones in a 400° F oven for one or two hours. Deglaze roaster and place bones and drippings in a large pot, add celery, onion, carrot, bay leaves, and water to cover. Bring to a boil and simmer for four to six hours, adding liquid when needed. (You may prefer to refrigerate after the stock has simmered for a shorter period, then reboil and simmer it for the remainder of the time, allowing for a shorter preparation period on serving day.) When it has simmered for at least six hours, remove the large bones and vegetables. Strain the liquid through a fine mesh sieve and place the stock in the refrigerator overnight.

Remove fat from the surface and freeze, either in ice cube trays, or in 1- or 2-cup containers.

BEER — Used in cooking, beer adds a distinct flavor. It also increases the lightness of battered, fried foods. You can keep leftover beer, opened, in the refrigerator. Flat beer is wonderful in cheese soup, and you can add flat beer to enhance beef stock in stews.

BEETS — This cousin to spinach can be stored in the refrigerator for as long as two weeks; the tops, however, can become flavorless, so use them sooner for optimum taste. The fresh tops can be used as salad greens.

BERRIES — Store them, unwashed, in the refrigerator or rinse and freeze them in containers for later use.

BEURRE MANIE — This is a combination of equal parts softened butter and flour (2 tablespoons of each, combined, will thicken 1 cup of liquid). You can store it, refrigerated, up to one month.

BISCUITS — Biscuits can be frozen for as long as three months; they can be kept, well wrapped, in the dry pantry up to a week.

BLACK BEANS (often called turtle beans) — gaining popularity in rice dishes, salads, and soups; available dried

BLANCHE — This process is often used in preparing vegetables for freezing. Blanching stops the enzymatic processes within vegetables or fruits and sets the color and flavor. Blanching is also used for precooking fruit in juice and for aiding in the removal of skins and peels of vegetables, fruits, and nuts. See time chart in APPENDIX.

BONES — Make assorted stocks from all leftover bones, along with frozen leftover meats and poultry skins. See specific stocks — beef, ham, chicken, veal and fish — for directions.

BORAGE - This herb, with a faint cucumber flavor, grows easily in your kitchen herb garden. Use the flowers — candied — to garnish cakes, salads, fruit. To preserve, pick flowers fresh, with stem intact. Poke them through a flat mesh screen, paint blossoms with beaten egg white, then sprinkle with superfine sugar. Dry for 48 hours in a cool place, treat again with egg white and sugar, dry, then place in a shallow box. They will keep for four to six months in the dry pantry.

BOUILLABAISSE — This hearty fish soup can be stored no longer than three days in the refrigerator or two months in the freezer.

BOUILLON (consommé) — This clear stock is derived from meat and poultry. Available canned or in powder or cubes, homemade is the most flavorful and nutritious, and it has less sodium. Strain homemade beef stock through cloth until clear, or clarify chicken stock to make consommé. Use beef bouillon in cooking carrots or potatoes as a side vegetable for any beef dish; add a tablespoon brown sugar and a dollop of butter to bouillon prior to cooking vegetables to create a delicious side dish; serve it as an entrée with rice or noodles. Use chicken bouillon to steam rice and vegetables for added flavor, as well as for a delicious change.

BOUQUET GARNI — This traditional herb packet is used to flavor most meat and fish dishes, as well as various soups and sauces. To make your own — for your own use or for gifts — cut 4 to 6 inch squares of thin cotton fabric or cheesecloth; in the center, place fresh herbs, such as parsley, sage, bay leaves, thyme, marjoram; tie them in a bundle with string or unwaxed dental floss. Add the packet, while cooking, to the liquids of a dish, then remove and discard after use. A tea strainer which closes in on itself is another handy home use container for a quick bouquet garni. See also HERBS.

BRANDY — This spirit is distilled from fermented grape wines and other fruits and juices. Cognac is the highest quality of wine liqueur; however, there are many other brandies which one would choose to use in cooking, since Cognac is very expensive and can be very extravagant for a cooking ingredient. You can use brandy in any dish which calls for wine; however you must cut the amount by half when substituting brandy; also, brandy should be added earlier in the cooking process to allow the alcohol time to cook down.

BRAZIL NUTS — See NUTS.

BREAD — This product freezes well for long term storage (for as long as three months) and will store on the dry pantry shelf for three to five days, before deteriorating. It can be stored for as long as two weeks in the refrigerator, but the bread may absorb refrigerator odors. Save all bread trimmings and leftovers in a bag in your freezer, until you have enough to make homemade crumbs. Let the breads thaw at room temperature, then put them in a food processor to make fine bread crumbs.

BREAD CRUMBS — These will store well on the dry pantry shelf for weeks if they are sealed tightly; optimum storage — several months — is in the refrigerator, providing you allow no moisture to infiltrate your container. One slice of bread or toast should yield 1/3 cup crumbs. Use fine dry crumbs underneath the crust of pies which you intend to freeze or in which you plan to use moist fillings; it will help keep the crust from getting soggy. Make Italian crumbs by adding herbs, seasonings, and dry grated Parmesan cheese. For buttered crumbs, toss 1 teaspoon melted butter with 1 cup soft bread crumbs.

BREAD DOUGH — Although it freezes well, it is better to bake breads, then freeze, because it is more difficult for frozen dough to reach the proper rising temperature. Try using potato water when making yeast breads; it adds moisture, volume, and texture, as well as acting as a natural preservative.

BREAD STUFFING — Use this product within three to five days if it's stored in the refrigerator; it can be frozen for two or three months. Reheat directly from frozen state; thawing at room temperature can allow toxins to grow. Never leave stuffing inside the cavity of poultry.

BRINE — This salty solution is used in preserving foods. Make brine fresh before use. Recipe for light brine is: 4 cups water and 1 tablespoon salt.

BROCCOLI — This vegetable will store in the hydrator tub of your refrigerator for up to two weeks. When flowerets begin to lighten in color, the vegetable is losing freshness and food value. Broccoli freezes well; see "Appendix: Pantry Charts and Tables" for blanching instructions.

BROWN SUGAR — Store, tightly sealed, in the dry pantry for as long as one year. See also SUGAR. Substitution: 1 cup less 2 tablespoons white sugar; stir into 1/4 cup molasses. Let stand one hour and use as brown sugar.

BROWNING — Add 1/2 teaspoon caramelized sugar to the fat in which you brown meats; the color will be richer, and the sugar will add nice flavor.

BRUSSELS SPROUTS — You can store this vegetable in the hydrator tub of the refrigerator for two weeks. Nutmeg is an excellent seasoning for Brussels sprouts; cheese is the ideal accompaniment.

BUTTER — It freezes well, as long as two months at 0° F, and will keep in the refrigerator for two to three weeks at maximum food quality. Make your own seasoned, whipped butter; bring butter to room temperature, beat with mixer (or processor) until light and fluffy; add garlic oil, herbs, or seasonings and store, tightly covered, in the refrigerator. Substitution: To equal 1 cup butter in cooking, add 1/2 teaspoon salt to 1 cup margarine or 7/8 cup lard. See also FLAVORED BUTTER categories.

BUTTERBALLS — See HERBAL BUTTERBALLS.

BUTTERMILK (also called sour milk) — Store it in the refrigerator no longer than one week past the manufacture date on the package. Substitutions: For 1 cup buttermilk, combine 1 tablespoon vinegar and enough sweet milk to equal 1 cup; let stand 5 minutes; or combine 1 3/4 teaspoon cream of tartar and 1 cup evaporated milk. Another substitution for 1 cup of buttermilk is 3/4 cup plain yogurt and 1/4 cup reconstituted nonfat dry milk.

### -C-

CABBAGE — The cabbage family includes red, green, savoy, and Chinese cabbages, as well as broccoli, cauliflower, kale, and kohlrabi. It keeps well in the refrigerator for two weeks. Before using cabbage in recipes which will be cooked or baked, parboil cabbage for five minutes, drain and proceed with the recipe. Add vinegar — 1 tablespoon to 2 cups cooking liquid — to red cabbage to help retain its bright color; you may use lemon juice instead, if you prefer.

CAJUN SPICE — Purchase this ingredient ready-made or combine 1 teaspoon black pepper, 1 teaspoon paprika, 1/2 teaspoon garlic salt, and 1/4 teaspoon ground allspice for a last minute recipe. See also SPICES AND SPICED SEASONINGS.

CAKE — You can freeze an iced layer cake (or portion of it) if you wrap it carefully, though it is better to freeze cake without icing. Reserve cake crumbs in a freezer bag to add to any dessert toppings such as crumb topping on coffee cake; such cake crumbs may also be used on the bottom of pie plates in order to keep the crust flaky, when you plan to use very liquid fillings. You can substitute buttermilk in any cake recipe that calls for regular milk; just add 1/4 teaspoon of baking soda to the dry ingredients for every 1/2 cup buttermilk you use. This makes your cakes incredibly light. Add powdered anise to the dry ingredients of sponge cake to improve the bland flavor.

CANDIED FRUIT (glazed) — Cook fruit, fruit peel, or ginger slowly (approximately one or two hours) in heavy sugar syrup, until the fruit is plump and translucent, then drain and dry it. It will store on the dry pantry shelf for months if tightly sealed. It will keep in the freezer for one year.

CANNED FOODS — Most canned foods are recommended for best storage as long as one year; exceeding that time doesn't mean the food inside has spoiled, but losses are possible in texture value, flavor and nutrients. As long as the can is not bulging or leaking, it is safe to use. *Always* wipe the top of cans before opening; the stores often have the cans sprayed with insecticides, and there is usually some dust accumulation. Try not to throw out liquids from canned goods. Retain a few large plastic containers in the freezer — one for vegetable juices, one for fruit juices, one for seafood juices. (Pour meat and poultry drainings into your frozen stock containers.) In canned foods, there are a lot of water soluble nutrients, which you will be losing down the drain if you don't have a reserve container. Instead of water listed in a recipe for a dessert, use reserved fruit liquids; a fruit beverage can also be substituted for water. Utilize reserved vegetable liquids when blanching fresh vegetables (except for cabbage or Brussels sprouts), or use the liquid for casseroles, stews, and soups. In developing a habit of reserving these liquids, you will reap the benefits of better flavor and nutrition, as well as creating less waste.

CANNELLINI BEANS — See WHITE CANNELLINI BEANS.

CAPERS — These pickled flower buds originate on a shrub which grows predominantly in western Europe. Available at most markets in both large and small buds, the smallest are the most flavorful. They are used in meat sauces, salads and antipastos, adding "instant gourmet" to any dish.

CAPSICUM PEPPERS — These include pimentos, chili peppers, cayenne peppers, paprika peppers and bell peppers. Store fresh peppers in the refrigerator, unwrapped, for as long as one week after purchase. Always wear gloves when handling chili peppers to avoid burning your skin or eyes. You may store dried peppers in the dry pantry for one to two years.

CARAMEL - The recipe is: 1 tablespoon sugar to 1 tablespoon water, heated until water evaporates and sugar begins to brown. This will give you a small amount of true caramel sugar to use in browning meats and flavoring stocks, soup, or gravy. Crystallize caramel in your food processor for sprinkling over foods. You can double the recipe if needed; it stores in the dry pantry for one month.

CARAMELIZED SUGAR — See CARAMEL and PRALINE POWDER.

CARAWAY — See HERBAL SEASONINGS and SEEDS.

CARD FILE — Keep a recipe box in your dry pantry for note keeping. One section could be titled "Shopping," for keeping records and receipts for future comparison. Another section could be "Entertaining"; this gives you a place to put recipes you wish to try on friends or relatives (perhaps dishes which you wouldn't necessarily make on an every day basis); other items included in the entertainment section might be an individual card for each person, couple, or group you have entertained in your home, noting what you served on what date. This way you won't find yourself serving the same dish twice to the same party. Another important section could be "Pantry Inventory"; here you could keep track of purchases and future needs to reference before you shop. Start with these and you'll find yourself filling the box with even more ideas and sections which help you use your pantry to its most diverse potential.

CARROTS — Store them in the hydrator tub of the refrigerator for as long as two weeks. Cut off the sprout ends before storing, in order to prevent flavor and nutrient loss. You may utilize the commonly-discarded carrot peelings, ends and tops when preparing stocks for other foods. To make carrot curl garnishes, slice carrots with a vegetable peeler, then place the strips in ice water for 5 minutes.

CASSEROLES — Prepared casseroles will keep in the refrigerator for as long as five days, depending on individual contents; they will keep in the freezer for as long as three months. Never thaw casseroles at room temperature. When planning to freeze any casserole, line the container with aluminum foil. Place food contents in the lined container and freeze. When solid, remove foil and food from container, wrap the food well and put it back into the freezer. When ready to use, simply put the frozen food back into the original container and thaw. This practice will save a lot of valuable space in the freezer.

CASSIS — See Chapter 9, "A Larder of Extracts, Liqueurs, and Spirits."

CAULIFLOWER — This vegetable can store in the hydrator tub of the refrigerator for two weeks. When the curds (or flowerets) begin to brown, this signals aging. To limit this browning to a minimum, store flowerets in water which has a little sugar and vinegar added to it. An 8- to 10-minute parboil will reduce the gaseous quality of this vegetable, and you can add 1 teaspoon lemon juice or 1/2 teaspoon cream of tartar to keep the curds white while cooking.

CAVIAR — This product, which is sturgeon or salmon roe, has a delicate flavor and texture. It is available in tins or jars, with a shelf life of up to one year in the dry pantry, for optimum flavor.

CELERIAC — Keep this vegetable in the hydrator tub of the refrigerator for as long as two weeks. Do not freeze.

CELERY — Celery will store in the hydrator tub of the refrigerator optimally for two weeks. When stalks begin to go limp, slice them to smaller scale and place them in lightly salted water for longer storage. Before storing fresh celery stalks, trim off tops, bottoms, and leaves. Place these in your vegetable container in the freezer for making stocks another day. For dressing up vegetable beverages such as tomato juice, cut stalks of celery to one inch longer than the height of a glass, slash down from top of stalks in a varied manner, (approximately 5 to 8 slashes); place stalks in ice water in the glass for 1/2 hour to create celery curls for stirrers.

CEREAL GRAINS — bran, farina, grits, hot cereal mixes, oats, wheat flakes, wheat germ. Store these, tightly sealed, in the dry pantry; exceptions are bran and wheat germ, which should be stored in the refrigerator. The shelf life of cereal grains is approximately one year.

CEREALS — After purchasing cereal products, those which you plan to store long term in your dry pantry should be taken from plastic or paper bags and placed in sealable containers. Storage time is approximately two or three months. You can use appropriate cereal products as bread crumbs if necessary; place the cereals (fruited ones, of course, would not apply) in the processor or blender. You can restore crispness to shelved cereals by pouring onto a cookie sheet and placing in a 250° F oven for 10 minutes.

CHARD — See SWISS CHARD.

CHEESE — Hard cheese may be stored for as long as nine weeks in the refrigerator; soft cheese should be used within ten days of purchase. When you perforate the airtight seal on hard cheeses, it is best to rewrap the cheese with cling wrap before placing it back in the refrigerator. If any molds appear on hard cheeses, just scrape or cut them off; the cheese is still good. You can freeze cheddar, Swiss, all French cheeses, Greek, and most Italian cheeses for three to six months and still retain flavor with minimal crumbling. Cream and cottage cheese freeze well, but after freezing they must be used in cooking only; the texture changes which occur after thawing are irrelevant to the final dish. If you harden Swiss or cheddar cheese before grating — by exposing it to air or uncovering it in the refrigerator — it will make a finer grate. Another method is to wrap cheese slices consecutively with paper towels and then press to remove excess oil and calories. Spray the grater with vegetable oil spray before using; clean-up will be a breeze. Add grated cheeses to hot dishes just before serving, to reduce stringiness. For a quick topping to vegetables, sprinkle grated gruyere or Swiss over the top, prior to serving.

CHEESECAKE — Cheesecake can be refrigerated for two weeks; it freezes well for six months.

CHEESECAKE TOPPING — Keep topping in the refrigerator for as long as one week or in the freezer for as long as three months. For topping brownies, cookies, cheesecakes, and pastries before baking, make your own recipe by simply adding 2 tablespoons of your favorite liqueur — such as crème de cocoa, crème de menthe, Amaretto or Frangelica — to 8 ounces cream cheese and 1 teaspoon vanilla; mix well and store in airtight containers until needed.

CHERRIES — Store unwashed in the refrigerator. Light colored cherries are best for cooking.

CHESTNUTS — See NUTS.

CHICKEN — You may store well-wrapped chicken in the refrigerator for no more than two days. Keep raw chicken away from cooked foods. (Cleanse any surface with which raw chicken has come in contact with a water and bleach solution of 10 parts water to 1 part bleach.) Whole chickens can be frozen for twelve months; cut-up, the pieces can be frozen for four to eight months. Reserve and use all chicken parts which you might normally throw away — such as bones, skins, feet and juices — to use in making your own chicken stock; see CHICKEN STOCK for instructions. Use salt sparingly when roasting or baking chicken, for the salt will release all the juices, making the meat dry. Season all poultry the day before you cook it, and the flavors will completely permeate the meat. Tarragon is the ideal herb for seasoning chicken. Mix the tarragon with a little white wine or vermouth (1 teaspoon tarragon to 1/2 cup wine) and you have the perfect chicken marinade. Let it sit for 1/2 hour to commingle, then add it to chicken. For a crisper broiled or baked chicken, rub imitation mayonnaise over the surface prior to cooking.

CHICKEN LIVERS — Accumulate chicken livers that come with chickens which you purchase; keep the livers in a freezer bag until you have enough for a meal. They will freeze well for six months. Cook the chicken livers in *hot* fat first, to seal juices and flavor; remove from fat and sauté in an appropriate medium, such as olive oil or butter. To prevent the liquids from curdling while you are making gravy from the drippings, add 1/2 teaspoon lemon juice to the pan and stir well before adding milk, water or roux.

CHICKEN STOCK — Gather approximately 3 pounds chicken bones and parts in a large stock pan and cover with water. Bring to a boil for 10 minutes, skim any foam that may rise, then add 4 to 6 carrots chopped into large pieces (or use your reserved carrot and vegetable pieces from the freezer), 4 to 6 celery stalks (chopped), 2 yellow onions (peeled and chopped), approximately 1 teaspoon salt and 1/2 teaspoon pepper. Simmer for two hours, strain and refrigerate. Freeze the stock in 2-cup portions for best utilization; it will keep for months. This recipe makes approximately 2 to 3 quarts.

CHICORY — This popular salad green should be kept in the refrigerator in a plastic bag which has a paper towel or cloth at the bottom to absorb moisture.

CHILI PASTE — This thick paste is made of mild chilies with a spicy, peppery influence for seasoning; it often comes with either garlic or other redolent flavorings necessary to certain recipe needs.

CHILI POWDER — See SPICES AND SPICED SEASONINGS.

CHILI SAUCE — See CONDIMENTS.

CHILI SEASONING — Make your own chili seasoning and store it in the dry pantry. To 2 tablespoons chili powder add: 1 tablespoon seasoned salt, 2 teaspoons cumin, 1 teaspoon oregano, 1 teaspoon salt, 1 teaspoon onion powder and 1/2 teaspoon garlic powder. Mix and store in airtight container. Use 2 tablespoons of seasoning per 6 servings of chili prepared.

CHILIES — See PEPPERS.

CHIVES — A member of the onion (lily) family, this ingredient is included often as an herb in cooking. Store chives, wrapped, in the refrigerator for as long as two weeks.

CHOCOLATE — For baking, bitter, semi-sweet, and unsweetened will store in the dry pantry for as long as two years. Milk chocolate has a twelve-month shelf life. Use a potato peeler to make chocolate curls with either semi-sweet or bitter chocolate. Chocolate which you have completely melted should be kept in the pan over warm water until ready to use. For a quick icing over fresh baked cupcakes, try sprinkling a few chocolate chips on top just before the cupcakes are done; put them back into the oven for the final 3 to 5 minutes of cooking time, then spread the melted chocolate over the tops after removing from the oven. Substitutions: For 1 ounce baking chocolate, use 1/4 cup powdered cocoa to 1 teaspoon butter or oil. Carob is not an equivalent substitute for cocoa.

CHOUX PASTE — See PATÉ A CHOUX.

CHUTNEY — Once opened, this product should be stored in the refrigerator pantry for no longer than one year. See RELISHES.

CILANTRO — Leaves of the coriander plant, this product is used as a main herb in salsa and Mexican dishes. Store as parsley, in the refrigerator for as long as two weeks or in the freezer — after the leaves are washed and dried — for as long as four months.

CINNAMON — See SPICES.

CINNAMON SUGAR — Keep this ingredient in an airtight container in the dry pantry. Add 2 tablespoons cinnamon to 1 cup white granulated sugar.

CLAM CHOWDER — If you are shucking your own clams for chowder, do not discard the water used to boil them; strain the water carefully through a very fine sieve (being careful not to disturb the sand on the bottom of the pot) into another pot; use this liquid as your stock. Add any juices you may have reserved from canned seafoods; you will be amazed at the flavor you can attain. Note: salt pork tastes much better than bacon in making chowder.

CLAMS — Hardshell clams, cherry stones, littlenecks, softshelled, steamers, and razor clams are the most available ones found in the U.S. Fresh, they can store in the refrigerator for two weeks if they are unopened. However, for optimum flavor as well as bacterial retardation, it is better to de-shell and freeze them for later use, if you need to keep them for longer than one week. Opened, clams are able to keep for no longer than twelve hours. These clams have a great deal of sand. You can release this sand by soaking them in a mixture of 1 gallon water to 1/3 cup salt; let stand undisturbed for one hour. Throw out the water after removing the clams. Place them in a new container to either make steamers or prepare for chowder; cover them, bringing to a boil and removing clams as they just open. Reserve the cooking juices by allowing them to settle; pour off the broth, being careful not to disturb the bottom settlings; strain through a sieve and use for seafood stock later.

CLARIFIED BUTTER — Melt butter over low heat in a heavy saucepan; do not stir. When completely melted, there will be a layer of clear liquid butter atop a milky layer. Carefully pour off or siphon the clear liquid and discard the milky residue. The clear liquid is clarified butter.

COARSE SALT — Keep a supply of large grain salt for various culinary needs, such as for garnishing special breads (sprinkled on top) or making effective brines. Coarse salt is also called kosher salt.

COCOA — Since cocoa is a pure product containing its own natural preservative, it will stay for many years stored on your dry pantry shelf. Substitution: 1/4 cup cocoa to 1 teaspoon butter or oil, to equal 1 square of chocolate. To avoid the skin that forms on freshly made cocoa, beat the liquid to a frothy stage immediately after removing from the stove.

COCONUT MILK — This is made by grating the flesh of fresh coconut and scalding it with warm water. The resulting liquid is the "milk." Coconut "water" is the fluid inside a fresh coconut.

COFFEE — Store opened containers of coffee beans or ground coffee in the refrigerator or freezer; this prevents the oil from evaporating, thus preserving the rich flavor. Pour leftover coffee into ice cube trays and freeze for iced coffees; this helps not only the flavor of the beverage but keeps it from being diluted as the cubes melt.

COLD CUTS — Keep sliced meats, wrapped well, in the refrigerator for no longer than one week. Freeze cold cuts immediately after purchase for longer storage, for as long as three months.

CONDIMENTS — These are prepared sauces, liquids and seasonings which are added to foods during or after cooking to enhance the flavor. Store them on a shelf of the dry pantry until they are opened, then store them in the refrigerator, if the package suggests, for as long as one year.

CONFECTIONER'S SUGAR — See SUGAR.

CONSOMMÉ — This clear, flavored liquid is used to make aspics and gelatins and can be interchanged with bouillon. Use 1 tablespoon unflavored gelatin to 2 1/2 cups consommé to make a standard aspic or gelatin base. To make consommé that gels naturally, use a proportionate amount of veal or beef knuckles in the stock preparation which you boil down to make consommé. For chicken consommé, you can add the cleaned and cut feet of the bird — prepared by your butcher — to your stock as you simmer, thus allowing this clear stock to gel naturally.

COOKIES — You can store fresh made cookies in the dry pantry for as long as a week in tightly sealed containers. In the freezer, cookie dough can be stored for up to three months; frozen cookies will last for one or two months; tightly wrap both dough and cookies, in order to prevent drying out. Most recipes call for all-purpose flour when making cookies. When making oatmeal cookies, toast the grains in the oven for 10 minutes in a low temperature oven before adding to the recipe ingredients; this will add a nutty flavor to the final cookies.

COOKING (PREPARATION) DAY — Try to schedule a day when you can devote an afternoon or morning to preparing stocks, casseroles, side dishes and baked goods or to attending fresh vegetables and fruits. Once you reap the benefits of this minimal effort, you will wish to incorporate the "cooking day" concept into your regular routine. A little planning is all it takes — a block of two to four hours is all you need!

CORN — For maximum flavor, try to use corn on the cob the day you purchase it. If you must store this food for a few days, stand the ears stem side down in a pan of shallow water to maintain freshness.

For long-term storage, a few weeks in the refrigerator will prevent the sugars in corn from turning starchy; however, it is best to blanche the corn, remove from the husks and freeze (see BLANCHING). To intensify the flavor of fresh cooked corn on the cob, add a few of the husks to the cooking water. Try roasting fresh corn on the cob in a 325° F oven for approximately 45 minutes, having removed the silks and leaving the husks. This method yields an enticing dish.

CORN GRAINS — polenta, white cornmeal, blue cornmeal, yellow cornmeal. Store in dry pantry, tightly sealed, as long as one year.

CORNICHONS — These are also known as sour gherkins. See PICKLES.

CORNISH HENS — See POULTRY.

CORN FLOUR (masa) — milled cornmeal; see Corn Grains

CORNMEAL — Stone ground corn is made from the whole corn and is more nutritious than the granular corn meal which we often purchase at the market. However, stone ground should be stored in the refrigerator or freezer, because the germ is present and contains natural fat.

CORNSTARCH — This ingredient imparts a clear quality when used for thickening gravy, sauces, and soups, as opposed to flour, which can be opaque. Use 1 teaspoon cornstarch to 1/2 cup liquid for a medium sauce. For other thickening uses, when recipes call for 2 tablespoons of flour to thicken a preparation, you can substitute 1 tablespoon cornstarch. Store indefinitely in the dry pantry. See THICKENERS.

CORN SYRUP — See SYRUPS.

COURT BOUILLON — This liquid, used for poaching fish, is a combination of enough water to cover the fish, with carrot, onion and herbs and either wine, vinegar or lemon juice; these ingredients are combined and brought to a boil prior to adding the fish. (Use 2 tablespoons wine, vinegar or lemon juice for every 1/2 cup of water.) Use wine or lemon juice in court bouillon for poaching salmon. Vinegar is preferred for shellfish. To make a large amount of court bouillon, sauté in a large saucepan: 2/3 cup chopped onion, 2/3 cup chopped carrots and 2/3 cup chopped celery in 1/2 stick melted, unsalted butter for 5 minutes. Add 1 cup dry white wine and 8 cups water; simmer for 20 minutes. (You can reuse court bouillon by straining carefully and freezing.)

COUSCOUS — This cereal-grained pasta can be stored in the dry pantry.

CRAB — Use crab as quickly as possible after its purchase for maximum flavor and freshness. You can freeze crab meat for three months. Canned crab meat is useful in cooking; retain drained liquids in your freezer with other fish stock or seafood liquids for use in making soups, court bouillon or chowder. To improve the flavor of canned crab meat, soak the meats in icy water for 2 or 3 minutes; this removes any canned taste.

CRACKERS — Crackers stored in the dry pantry will stay fresh and crispy for two to three months, if properly wrapped. Stale crackers can be ground into fine crumbs for use in ground meat dishes, and in coatings and toppings for vegetable dishes. Graham crackers can be ground for use in making pie and cheesecake crusts; 18 crackers equals approximately 1 1/2 cups crumbs.

CRANBERRIES — See BERRIES.

CREAM — Cream is available in varying degrees of milkfat. Here, listed from highest milkfat content to the lowest are: heavy whipping cream, light whipping cream, coffee cream, half and half.

Storage in your *Perishables Pantry* may be as long as two weeks or until the date on the carton. If you purchase cream for use later, you may freeze it for three to six months. Thaw heavy whipping cream in the refrigerator, then whip. You can use cream in cooking, even if you are not certain of its freshness, by adding a pinch of baking soda to the cream before adding to any hot liquids or dishes; this prevents curdling. Evaporated milk can be substituted for light cream in cooking, if you're counting calories. For quick dessert toppings, put leftover whipped cream on a baking sheet in small heaps, then put them in the freezer. When they are solid, place the heaps in a plastic bag and seal. They thaw in 10 or 15 minutes, ready for use.

CREAM CHEESE — See CHEESE.

CREAM PIES — will store in the refrigerator for approximately three to five days

CREAM PUFFS - These can be frozen after baking, but not after filling. See PATÉ A CHOUX.

CRÈPES - These are best when they're fresh-made, but they do freeze well when they're wrapped between sheets of waxed paper to separate. Mix your crèpe batter about an hour prior to cooking; let it sit in the refrigerator to cool. With this method, the crèpes will have a much smoother texture.

CROQUETTES — Similar to a fritter, these are delicate morsels, made of approximately 2 cups dried or minced solids (which can be anything from fish to rice) to 1 cup cream or white sauce. They're then formed into cones or balls and coated lightly before deep frying. Crushed potato chips make an excellent coating for fish croquettes. You can store leftover croquettes for three days in the refrigerator or one month in the freezer. Bake to reheat for 15 minutes in a 350° F oven.

CROUTONS — If properly wrapped and sealed, croutons will store for as long as three months in the dry pantry. Make your own by dicing day-old bread and tossing with butter which has been seasoned with your favorite herbs or spices; bake them on a cookie sheet for 15 minutes in a moderate oven. Remove from the oven and toss with Parmesan. Fresh croutons may be frozen for as long as six months. Thaw them at room temperature before toasting in the oven, prior to use.

CUCUMBERS — These will store in the refrigerator for two weeks, but using them within one week is better. Cucumbers tend to get soft easily. When cucumbers are abundant, you can freeze the pureed cucumber meats for use later in fish sauces, salad dressings, meat sauces, and soup. Peel six cucumbers, cut lengthwise and remove seeds. Place in saucepan, sprinkle with 1 teaspoon salt and add 1/4 cup boiling water. Simmer for 10 minutes, pass through a sieve or food mill and place in small containers — one-cup size — to freeze for as long as three months.

CUPCAKES — Frosted, they will store on a shelf for one week, if snugly covered. Wrapped tightly to prevent frost, they may be frozen for three months. (Do not remove muffin paper if planning to freeze.) To make wrapping easier, sprinkle hard candies over the frosting; this will keep the tops from adhering to the plastic wrap. To make quick frosting for cupcakes, sprinkle either chocolate, peanut butter, or other flavored chips over tops straight from the oven. Allow topping to melt — replacing them in the oven for two to three minutes — then spread. See also MUFFINS.

CURRY — See SPICES.

CURRY BUTTER — This is good to have on hand to toss into pasta or melt over freshly steamed seafood. Combine 1/2 cup butter, 2 tablespoons lemon juice, 1 tablespoon each chopped parsley and curry powder, and 1/2 teaspoon minced garlic. This can be refrigerated for two weeks or frozen for six months.

CURRY PASTE — Available at Asian markets, this thick greenish paste is used as a curry seasoning.

CUSTARD — Store custard no longer than three to five days maximum; put it into the refrigerator immediately after cooking and cooling. You cannot freeze custards, custard pies, or custard filled desserts.

**-D-**

DAIKON — This white radish can be stored in the refrigerator for two weeks.

DAIRY PRODUCTS — See specific types.

DANDELION GREENS — Purchase only tender young greens, for the older greens are bitter and tough. They will store in the refrigerator for two weeks when placed in a plastic bag which has paper toweling in the bottom to absorb excess moisture.

DASHEEN — See TARO.

DATES — When dried, dates will keep in the dry pantry for as long as a year, or until the package date. For easier handling when chopping or cutting dates for recipes, freeze them first. Coat chopped dates (or any sticky fruit) with flour before adding to recipes to prevent the fruit from settling.

DEHYDRATED FRUITS — Store these in airtight containers in a dark, cool place for as long as two years.

DEHYDRATED VEGETABLES — Store them tightly in the dry pantry to prevent their humidifying; they can be stored indefinitely this way. Rehydrate according to package directions, or soak them in liquids for about half an hour before use.

DESSERT SAUCES — These include: custard sauces, which can be refrigerated for three days, but *never* frozen; chocolate sauces, which can be refrigerated for two to three months; liqueur sauces, which also can be refrigerated; fruit sauces, which can be made up as needed from frozen fruit purees. You can purchase ready-made fruit sauces and store them indefinitely in the dry pantry, as long as they remain unopened.

DILL — See HERBS.

DOUGH — See specific types.

DOUGHNUTS — When tightly wrapped, these will store in the dry pantry for as long as a week before turning stale; fresh doughnuts, tightly sealed, may be frozen for three to six months.

DRESSINGS — Fresh salad dressing is the basis for a great salad. With the broad availability of pre-made salad dressings, however, maintaining a wide assortment of favorite dressings in your refrigerator is easy, acceptable and time-saving. After opening, these will store in your refrigerator until the date on the container, or no longer than three months. See also VINAIGRETTE.

DRIED FRUITS — See specific types.

DUCK — Use fresh duck as soon as possible, storing it no longer than two days in the refrigerator. Due to its high fat content, it should not be frozen for more than six months.

DUCK FAT — Store it in the *Perishables Pantry* (the refrigerator) for no longer than two weeks.

DUXELLES — This is a type of mushroom preparation. See MUSHROOMS.

### -*E*-

ÉCLAIRS — See PATÉ A CHOUX.

EGGS — In order to discern how long you can store eggs in your refrigerator, check the date on the carton of eggs which you purchase or ask the dairy clerk for the date when the eggs were delivered. Most eggs will stay fresh for two weeks after delivery. Don't wash your eggs before storing, because this removes the natural sealant which prevents oxidation of the egg. You can check the freshness of eggs by floating them gently in a clear glass of water. If the egg sinks, it's fresh. Eggs are packaged with the wider end up, not to make them appear larger, but to keep the air bubble inside stationary. If you must remove the eggs from their carton to place in the refrigerator, store them in a container which allows them to remain with the small bottom of the egg down; they will stay fresh longer. Eggs can be frozen, in various forms, for up to four months. If you need to use up your supply of eggs before they spoil, beat them in a large bowl and add 1/2 teaspoon salt to every 1 cup beaten eggs. The salt helps to stabilize the eggs for freezing. Pour the egg mixture into an ice cube tray and freeze. Remove the frozen cubes and place them in a clear freezer bag, label, and date. One large cube equals approximately one egg, or slightly less. You can freeze hard boiled eggs; shred before placing them in a freezer container. Use them as a garnish for salads and soups or sprinkle them on sandwiches. You cannot freeze any dish which has a cooked egg-custard base, because the custards aren't stable. Substitution: For one egg you can use 3 tablespoons plus 1 teaspoon frozen eggs or 2 tablespoons frozen egg yolk plus 1 tablespoon milk. See also EGG WHITES, EGG YOLKS, CUSTARDS, MERINGUES, SAUCES, and THICKENERS.

EGG WHITES — Separated from yolks, egg whites can be stored, covered, in a glass container in your refrigerator for three days. For longer storage, you can freeze egg whites (no salt) in an ice cube tray.

One large cube equals approximately 1 1/2 egg whites or 3 tablespoons whites. Eight egg whites will make approximately one cup frozen whites. Be sure to remove frozen whites from cube tray, place in a sealable container, then label and date. Four months is the longest period for which you would want to freeze whites. Foods made with egg whites — such as angel food cake — freeze well. Whites separate from yolks much easier when cold, but for maximum whipping volume, allow the whites to come to room temperature before whipping. Frozen egg whites, thawed, and egg whites which are slightly aged (one to two weeks) whip better than fresh eggs when separated. This is so because the thinner whites of frozen and aged eggs allow larger air volume. When whipping a large number of whites for meringues and mousse, use 1/2 teaspoon salt per cup of whites (8 whites) to increase volume; add 1 teaspoon cream of tartar as a stabilizer. <u>Substitution</u>: For one egg white you can use 2 tablespoons thawed egg whites.

EGG YOLKS — You can store egg yolks in the refrigerator for three to five days by placing the yolks in a glass container and pouring a thin layer of cold water over the surface before sealing the container. Freeze yolks by adding 1 teaspoon salt to every cup of yolks before placing them in a cube tray. After they are frozen, remove them from the tray and place them in a freezer bag, label and date. One large cube approximates 2 or 3 yolks; there are 14 yolks per cup. Store yolks no longer than four months this way. Leftover egg yolks can be used in many ways, such as in making custards, bechamel sauce and mornay sauce or in using as a thickening agent in various soups and sauces. You can substitute egg yolks for whole eggs in recipes by simply adding a tablespoon of milk to make up for the lack of whites. Substitution: For one egg yolk, you can use 3 1/2 teaspoons thawed frozen yolks.

EGGPLANT — When purchasing this diverse vegetable, it is best to select those which are heavy, but not necessarily larger. Eggplants will store for two weeks at optimum freshness in the refrigerator.

ENCHILADA SAUCE — This product is available canned or in powder mix, but you can make your own by combining 1/3 cup vegetable oil, 1 crushed garlic clove and 3 tablespoons all purpose flour in a medium sauce pan. Cook the mixture over low heat, stirring until it is slightly browned. Dissolve 2 tablespoons chili powder in 1/3 cup hot water; stir into flour mixture. Add an additional 1 1/3 cups hot water to sauce and 1/2 teaspoon salt; simmer 5 minutes, stirring occasionally. This sauce will keep in the refrigerator, covered, for two weeks or in the freezer for six months.

ENGLISH MUFFINS — These can be stored for one week in the dry pantry, but they store better, frozen — for as long as three months. If they aren't already split, slice the muffins before freezing and position the cut edges so that all of them face the same direction; this facilitates separation while they are still frozen.

EQUIVALENTS — See specific item for equivalent and substitution information. Also see MEASURES.

ESPRESSO POWDER (instant) — Keep this product in the dry pantry. For a richer, deeper coffee bean flavor, use it in recipes which call for coffee granules.

EVAPORATED MILK — This product is whole milk from which half the water content has been removed. It is usually available fortified, canned. If you add an equal amount of water, you can use it in recipes as whole milk.

EXTRACTS — These are concentrated liquid flavoring substitutes, available in extensive varieties. The shelf life of extracts in the dry pantry is three to five years, due to the alcohol content, which acts as a preservative. <u>Substitutions</u>: Often you can use liqueur of the appropriate flavor instead of extract flavoring. You must increase the amount of liqueur, compared to extract, by half. See Chapter 9, "A Larder of Extracts, Liqueurs, and Spirits," for more information.

## -*F*-

FATS — Store cooking fats, such as that of bacon and duck, in the freezer for as long as three months. Lard can be stored safely at room temperature. Keep salad and cooking oils in a dark cupboard, at room temperature; nut oils and grain oils such as walnut oil do better when stored in the refrigerator. If clouding is present, allow the oil to come to room temperature before use. You can reuse vegetable fats used for deep frying; just strain oil through a sieve and refrigerate.

FENNEL — See HERBS.

FERMENTED BLACK BEANS — oriental preparation used in many dishes for pungent, salty, legume flavoring

FILBERTS (Hazelnuts) — See NUTS.

FINES HERBS — The use of this mixture of fresh herbs originated in French cuisine; the herbs are chopped fine for use in dishes as a bouquet garni, except that they aren't removed after cooking. The main herb used is chervil, with basil, tarragon, and parsley added as desired.

FIRE EXTINGUISHER — Keep an extinguisher near your kitchen or in your pantry for any flame eruptions in your kitchen — where most house fires originate. (For small, in-pan fires, simply place the lid on; the lack of oxygen will extinguish the fire.) Use baking soda to sprinkle over small flames on your burner.

FISH — Fresh fish is relatively odorless and can be kept in your refrigerator for one or two days. If the fish begins to have an odor, use it immediately, for the smell is an indication of deterioration. Freeze freshly purchased fish for longer storage, three to six months, in one of the following manners:

Glazing — Place clean fish on a tray in the freezer, allow to become solid, then dip fish in very cold water for 2 minutes and freeze on tray again. Repeat process one more time, then wrap, label, and store in the freezer.

Brine Method — Make a *brine* of 1 cup coarse salt to 4 quarts cold water. Soak fish in this liquid for approximately 10 minutes. Drain, wrap, label and freeze.

Ice Block Method — For smaller fish or cut up steaks and fillets from larger fish, this method works well to prevent freezer burn; however, it takes up more space than the other two methods. Place clean fish or meats in a loaf pan appropriately sized to the fish. Cover fish with ice water, (add a few sprigs of dill and a drop of lemon juice to the water; do not salt) and place in the freezer. When solid, remove ice block by gently warming underside of pan with warm tap water. Place ice block in foil, label and freeze.

Allow all frozen fish to thaw in the refrigerator. Use thawed fish immediately. You can extend the freezer life of your frozen fish to six months, maximum, by removing all visible fat before freezing. If you don't remove the fins and tails of the fish before cooking, you will find de-boning much easier, and you can use the bones to make fish stock or to enhance the flavor of your previously made supply of court bouillon or fish stock.

FISH SAUCE — This Oriental food condiment is indispensable in Thai and Vietnamese cooking.

Fish sauce is milder in saltiness than soy sauce. Keep it on a shelf of the dry pantry. See CONDIMENTS.

FISH STOCK — Bottled or canned fish stock from your dry pantry cannot equal the quality and flavor that homemade has; however, the bought items are preferred to water when you need a liquid equivalent for preparing fish or seafood dishes. To make your own, reserve bones and liquids from preparing fish dishes — or buy an assortment of fish parts which your butcher can prepare for you (no fats or fish heads) — and use them with the liquids which you have reserved from canned fish and seafoods. Place in a large stock pot, all solids, approximately 2 pounds of fish bones and leftover meats, 1 bay leaf, carrot, celery, 1/2 teaspoon salt, 1/4 teaspoon pepper, and enough water to cover, approximately 4-6 cups. Bring to a boil, then simmer, covered, for 30-45 minutes, then strain. (You can add 1/4 to 1/2 cup dry white wine for an added gourmet touch during the simmering process.) Fresh stock will keep in the refrigerator for six days, but frozen will last for six months. If you use and reuse your stock (thawing, using, straining, and refreezing) it will get better and better, and in six months time you can finish it off by making a spectacular *bouillabaisse* or chowder. You can make a fish glaze, which is basically rich fish stock reduced down to a thick, gel-like, caramel colored sauce. Bottle and keep it in the refrigerator or freezer to dilute for either stock or court bouillon. This saves space without losing quality.

FIVE SPICE POWDER — See SPICES AND SPICED SEASONINGS.

FLAMBÉ — This is the process of flaming a dish to enhance final flavor and presentation. Use brandy, vodka, or whiskey to flambé meats, poultry and fish; use cognac, liqueurs, or rum for flaming desserts.

FLAVORED BUTTERS — See HERBAL BUTTERBALLS or specific herb.

FLOUNDER — See FISH.

FLOUR — Store all-purpose and cake flours in your dry pantry; keep whole grain flours in the refrigerator or freezer. Seal flour containers tightly to prevent infestations of insects. See Chapter 11, "Pantry Pests."

FOIS GRAS — Fattened goose (or duck) liver is often seasoned with truffles and cognac and is usually found in paté form, in blocks.

FREEZING — Keep the temperature in your freezer at a constant 0° F in order to maintain the freezability of foods as indicated for that specific item. An average freezer will keep foods frozen for two days in case of power failure, if you do not open the door. Most partially thawed foods can be safely re-frozen, except for ice cream. Organize your freezer to help keep an inventory of items there; if you have only a small freezer, keep items that are to be frozen for only a short time close to the front so you don't leave them past their *due* date. Wrap snugly and label and date all freezer items. Use oven proof dishes for freezing so that the container will not break during re-heating or baking. For thawing most items, the surest way to proper thawing is to allow the item to thaw in the refrigerator; however, vegetables, casseroles and pies can be cooked or baked right from the freezing point. Lightly season any foods which you plan to freeze, but be aware that the saltiness of foods diminishes with freezing. See "Appendix: Pantry Charts and Tables," for a list of freezing times for most common food items. There is more specific information for freezing about each food under its own heading.

FRITTERS — This term refers to deep or pan fried foods made of many combinations of ingredients. Storage is best achieved by freezing for as long as three months, then baking from frozen in a 375° F oven for 10 to 15 minutes. Fritters become soggy when stored in the refrigerator.

FROSTING — Canned, prepared frosting may be stored as long as a year in the dry pantry. Freeze homemade frosting up to six months, depending on whether it's buttercream (three months) or plain, sugar frosting.

FRUIT — Because most fruits have a natural preservative on their peels, they should not be washed before storage. You can ripen raw fruits by placing them in paper bags with holes poked in them to allow the escape of ethylene gas. See specific fruit for more useful ideas and detailed information pertaining to storage.

FRUIT JUICE — Fruit juice concentrates may be safely frozen for as long as twelve months. In a container in the freezer, reserve all juices from any canned fruits you use. You can use these liquids as a base for a wonderful cake or dessert sauce by adding an appropriate amount of tapioca flour or cornstarch; these fruit liquids can also make any gelatin or baked dessert much more flavorful than if you use the plain water called for in the recipe.

FRUIT PEEL — Peel zest off of lemons, limes and oranges prior to squeezing or slicing them for use in recipes. Place zest in airtight containers; store it in the freezer for as long as one year. Candied peel can be stored in the dry pantry for six to twelve months.

FRUIT PUREE — You can store fruit puree in the refrigerator for two weeks or in the freezer for six months.

FRYING — For deep fat frying use vegetable and nut oils for best results. You can reuse the oils and fats after frying by straining them carefully and keeping them in the refrigerator. Once the oil or fat fails to produce fried foods with crisp golden crusts, it has been "fried out" and must be discarded.

FUDGE — After making, wrap it well and store it in the dry pantry for as long as two weeks. It freezes well, for as long as four months.

## -G-

GARBANZO (chick peas) — Store dried garbanzo beans in the dry pantry for as long as two years.

GARBANZO FLOUR (chick pea flour) — Store garbanzo flour, tightly covered, in the refrigerator.

GARLIC — Store fresh garlic in the dry pantry for as long as two weeks; after that time, peel the garlic bulbs (under hot water) and place them in a small jar of olive oil. Refrigerate for a week. You can use the garlic oil for making fresh salad dressing, or for sautéing. Another idea for using aging garlic bulbs is to add them to red or white vinegar for gifts or for home vinegar use. When sautéing garlic for recipes, do not brown it, for this gives a bitter taste to the garlic. You can also mince fresh garlic and place it in olive oil in the refrigerator to have handy during meal preparation. This will keep pungent for as long as two months.

GARLIC OIL — See GARLIC.

GARNISHES — Prepare and appropriately store assorted garnishes to enhance your prepared foods. Some examples are: toast points for paté, eggs for slicing, anchovy strips, olives, sun dried tomatoes, orange peel and slices, artichoke hearts, asparagus tips, capers, carrot curls, zucchini strips, chives, pimento, parsley, mushroom caps, truffles, gherkins, greens and radishes.

GELATIN — Keep a supply of unflavored gelatin on hand for use in cooking; also have on hand an assortment of flavored gelatins to make special desserts. A rule of thumb for gelatins is 1 tablespoon gelatin to 1 3/4 cups liquid. Be sure to dissolve the gelatin completely before adding to recipes. (Also see ASPICS.)

GERANIUM SUGAR — Used for making delicate cakes and desserts, geranium sugar should be stored in airtight containers in the dry pantry.

GINGER — See SPICES.

GINGER ROOT — Fresh ginger root can be stored in a plastic bag in your freezer for as long as two years. Simply take it out when needed and slice, frozen, or grate. Mince fresh ginger and keep it in olive or peanut oil in the refrigerator for as long as one month; this method keeps it on hand for ready use during meal preparation. You can candy ginger by slicing it into julienne strips and sautéing on low, in sugar syrup, until opaque. Let it drain and store it in a plastic container in your dry pantry.

GLAZE — This can be a fruit, fish, meat or poultry sauce. The liquids are slowly boiled down (reduced) until the water content is minimal and a rich, thick sauce results. Store these in the refrigerator as indicated under specific headings.

GLYCERIN — tasteless additive used in cooking for velvety texture

GNOCCHI — Store fresh gnocchi-style pasta in the refrigerator for as long as two weeks. Dried gnocchi can be stored in the dry pantry for two years.

GOOSE — Use fresh goose within two days or freeze, whole, for as long as six months. Goose has a high fat content, so you should poke the lower body of the goose with a fork before roasting or baking it, to allow fat to escape; turn the goose, rotisserie style, for even dispersing of juices.

GRAHAM CRACKERS — Store graham crackers in the dry pantry for as long as three months. You can use graham crackers — even stale ones — to make crumbs for use in pies and cheesecakes. One pound of graham crackers will yield approximately 4 cups of crumbs. Use a food processor or place crackers in a bag and roll a rolling pin over them.

GRAHAM SUGAR — To make graham sugar, crush 4 to 8 crackers (1/2 cup) and add 1 tablespoon sugar and 1 teaspoon cinnamon. Store this in airtight plastic bags or jars in the dry pantry for as long as three months.

GRANOLA — Store granola at room temperature in a sealed container for as long as two to four weeks. Make your own granola, starting with the basics: 2 cups oatmeal, 1 cup shredded coconut, 1/2 cup toasted wheat germ, 1/2 cup honey, and 1/4 cup cooking oil. Add such ingredients as nuts, raisins, dried apricots, dates and sesame seeds to your liking. Bake this for 45 minutes in a 300° F oven, stirring occasionally. Cool, stirring often to prevent lumping; seal in jars for storage in your dry pantry. For storage of more than two weeks, place in freezer bags and freeze for as long as twelve months; thaw it on a baking sheet at 300° F for 10 minutes.

GRAPEFRUIT — Store grapefruit in the hydrator tub of your refrigerator for as long as two weeks. Use hollowed out grapefruit skins (thicker peel is easier to use) as a garnish cup for desserts and as a fruit cup. Keep skins in ice water until ready to fill. For a decidedly different salad dressing, use grapefruit juice instead of vinegar.

GRAPE LEAVES — Store grape leaves in the refrigerator for as long as a month after opening. Use them for wrapping foods prior to cooking or baking.

GRAVY — Fresh gravy can be stored in the refrigerator for no more than two or three days. It is best to freeze leftover gravy in small containers or ice cube trays to use later; thawing is quick and easy. To freeze, allow gravy to cool and remove any fat that may come to the surface. Stir well, adding 1/4 teaspoon dry gelatin per cup of gravy (or white sauce) to prevent breakdown of emulsion, then place in freezing container. Depending on fat content, gravy can be frozen for one to three months. The gravies highest in fat content, such as beef or chicken, should be used sooner than those without a lot of fat. The leaner gravies are more stable and can take a longer freezing time.

GREEN SAUCE (not pesto) — Keep green sauce in your refrigerator for marinades, dips and salad dressings, as well as a sauce for chicken, seafood and pasta. To make your own; chop 1/4 pound fresh parsley (stems removed) and add 1/2 cup extra virgin olive oil, 3 cloves garlic (crushed), 1 tablespoon capers (drained), 1/2 teaspoon dried tarragon, and 3 tablespoons fresh lemon juice. Process in a blender or food processor until smooth. Keep in refrigerator, covered, for as long as a week; freeze for as long as three months. This recipe is good for topping steamed vegetables, grilled meats, fish, and seafood; it also can be mixed with 1/2 cup sour cream for a dip with crudities.

GREENS — These include beet greens, bok choy, Chinese chard, Swiss chard, chicory, collard greens, dandelion greens, kale, lettuces, mustard greens, spinach and turnip greens. Store them in the hydrator tub for three to seven days; freezing is possible with heartier greens for a longer storage time. Sauté the greens in their own juices for 2 or 3 minutes, place in storage bag and freeze for as long as twelve months. To prevent moisture buildup and decay of fresh greens, place a paper towel inside the bag or wrap greens in paper toweling before placing in plastic bags.

### -H-

HAM — Cured ham will keep well in the refrigerator much longer than other meats; wrapped well with most of the surface fat removed, a cured ham can be safely refrigerated for as long as two weeks. Frozen hams have a one-year perishability date. Reserve all of your fatty cuttings, as well as the bones of hams you serve, and make your own soup stock or ham glaze — see STOCK. Slice off a few thick portions of ham before you serve your meal; freeze them, after spreading them with a small amount of drippings or margarine, for use later in salads, scalloped potatoes or egg dishes. Canned hams slice easier if you chill them first. To glaze an unbaked ham, sprinkle the entire surface with vanilla sugar and bake at 450° F until brown; reduce to regular cooking temperature and proceed with regular cooking time (reduced — if necessary — by the time already cooked).

HAMBURGER — You can store ground beef in the refrigerator for as long as three days, unless the package date or odor indicate an earlier perishability. Ground meats have a higher spoilage rate than solid meats, due to the dispersed fat content. Hamburger can be frozen for four months; shape the meat into as flat a mound as possible for quicker freezing and maintenance. Thaw hamburger in the refrigerator. If you will be freezing hamburger for patties, season (except for salt) and shape the hamburger into patties *before* freezing; thawed ground meats do not hold together as well as fresh. To get the leanest possible ground meat without losing moistness, purchase ground round and add olive or rice bran oil. By using the leaner meat and substituting oils with lower cholesterol than the normal fat content of hamburger, you will be lowering the overall cholesterol level of all of your favorite hamburger dishes. You can extend ground meat and add flavor easily by using grated raw potatoes or dried potato flakes with a sprinkle of water or milk.

HARISSA — See SPICES AND SPICED SEASONINGS.

HASH — Hash can be stored in the refrigerator for two days, but the nature of hash, with its high fat content, makes deterioration swift. It can be frozen safely for three months. To make hash out of meat solids or leftovers, add an equal amount of diced potatoes (with a little onion) to shredded or diced meats. Add 1/3 as much gravy (or sauce) as there are solid ingredients.

HAZELNUTS (filberts) — See NUTS.

HERB BUTTER — Premixed herb butter can be stored in the refrigerator for two weeks. To make your own, allow 4 tablespoons butter to come to room temperature and add 2 teaspoons desired fresh minced herbs (1 teaspoon if using dried). Stir it well and place it in a covered container in the refrigerator for use on such foods as meat, poultry, fish and bread. You can freeze herb butter for as long as four months. See also HERBAL BUTTERBALLS.

HERB VINEGARS — Store herb vinegars in your dry pantry. You may purchase them or make your own by adding sprigs of desired herbs, such as tarragon, to a pint of white wine (or cider) vinegar. Allow to steep for two or three weeks before using. See also VINEGARS.

HERBAL BUTTERBALLS — Keep butterballs, wrapped well, in the refrigerator for as long as two weeks. They can be frozen for as long as six months. Make your own herbal butterballs using such ingredients as watercress, parsley, mint and chives to 1/2 cup unsalted butter at room temperature; mix 2 or 3 tablespoons fresh minced herbs to butter, salt and pepper to taste, 1 teaspoon lemon juice if desired, stir well, shape into balls and freeze. See also HERB BUTTER.

HERBS — Fresh herbs can be stored in the refrigerator for weeks if you wash and drain them well or spin them in a salad spinner, then place them in tightly closed containers. Most herbs freeze well, except for the stems, if you dry them thoroughly and keep them loosely packaged in airtight containers or freezer bags. Herbs can be kept in the freezer for six months without loss of pungency. When you're ready to use frozen herbs, do not thaw them; simply add them to your dish frozen, and they will thaw while cooking; this keeps them from losing their color. Dried herbs have a shelf life of four to eight months, depending a lot upon the conditions of the place where they are stored; exposure to light and moisture are detrimental. If your dried herb has lost its color and bouquet, it is probably stale in flavor as well. Grow your own fresh herbs in a shallow window box; plant the seeds in late winter or early spring and keep the earth moist. Clip fresh sprigs as needed. When you have an abundant crop — or have leftover bundles of parsley or other herbs — dry them by placing the washed and drained herbs in a paper bag and hanging them in your kitchen or pantry for seven to ten days. Gently shake the bag occasionally. If you purchase an herb (or spice) which you haven't used before, a rule of thumb to go by in seasoning foods is to start with 1/4 teaspoon and taste after a few minutes, repeating this process until the flavor you desire is reached; mark down the chosen amount on a card and keep it in your own file box under "Herbs and Spices" for future reference. Use fewer dried herbs (and spices) than the amount of fresh ingredients called for in recipes, since drying intensifies flavor; crush dried herbs and spices before adding to dishes, in order to break free the aromatic oils and flavors. When adding dried herbs to uncooked dishes, you may wish to soften them by soaking them for 10 or 15 minutes in any liquids called for in the recipe; another option is to boil the herbs in a small amount of water for one minute, strain, and proceed as if the herb were fresh. See also SPICES.

## HERBS AND THEIR COMPLIMENTS

Basil — tomato dishes, seafoods, vegetables, egg dishes, cheese sauces, curries

Bay Leaves — soups, stews, pot roasts, bouquet garni, grilling

Borage — salads, fish, seafood

Caraway — See HERBAL SEASONINGS AND SEEDS.

Chervil — egg soufflés, lamb, veal, pork, seafood, fines herbs

Chives — See HERBAL VEGETABLES.

Cilantro (coriander) — Mexican dishes, salsa, salads, herb butters

Dill — seafood, tomato dishes, cream sauces, salads, lamb, deviled eggs, vegetable.
Substitutions: You can interchange caraway seed, fennel seed and cumin seed for dill.

Fennel — See HERBAL SEASONINGS AND SEEDS.

Garlic — See HERBAL SEASONINGS AND SEEDS.

Lemon Balm — fish, seafood, salads, tea

Lemon Thyme — poultry, salads, seafood

Lemon Verbena — tomato dishes, salads, seafood sauces, tea

Lovage — seafood, casseroles, sour cream sauce, bouquet garni

Marigold — salads, legume soups, chowders, roast pork and veal, liver, rice, noodles

Marjoram — soups, seafood, poultry, vegetables, meats

Mint — sauces for lamb and veal, desserts, fruit cups, tea and other beverages

Oregano — tomato dishes, vegetables, meat loaf, stews

Parsley — tomato dishes, all meats, seafood, poultry, salads, garnishes, butters

Rosemary — legume soups, salmon, breads, poultry, meats, grilling

Sage — chowders and soups, poultry, pork, sausage, seafood, vegetables

Savory — green beans, legumes, soups, rice, pork, seafood, poultry

Sorrel — salads, eggs, cheese, fish, pesto

Spearmint — lamb, fruit salads, teas, lentils, poultry

Tarragon — poultry, butter sauces for meats and fish, lamb, seafood, fines herbs

Thyme — tomato dishes, cheese dishes, poultry stuffing, meats, vegetables, soup

## *HERBAL SEASONINGS AND SEEDS*

Anise — baked products, seafoods, fruits, salads, beverages

Capers — meat, poultry and seafood sauces, salads, tomato dishes

Caraway — cheese, cheese dishes, cabbage, vegetables, marinade, rice, pasta

Celery (leaves and seeds) — breads, meat loaves, seafoods, salads, sauces, tomato dishes

Cumin — curries, cheese, vegetable salads, butters, dressings

Fennel — fish, legume soups, tomato dishes, lamb

Juniper Berries — veal, lamb stew, game birds, venison, beverages

Mustard (seed and ground) — casseroles, legume soups, condiments

Nasturtium (leaves and flowers) — salads, garnish, red meats, butters

Poppy Seeds — cakes, cookies, breads, salad dressings, pasta

Sesame Seeds — canapes, breads, pasta, poultry, salads, salad dressing

## HERBAL VEGETABLES AND FRUITS

Chives — egg dishes, vegetables, seafood, condiments, garnish

Garlic (also powder and salt) — Italian, French, Mexican cooking, poultry, meats, sauces, soups

Horseradish — seafood, beef, salads, cocktail dressing, spreads

Lemon Peel — baking, beverages, sauces, seafoods, marinades

Mushrooms (dried) — soups, gravies, garnish, meats, salads

Onion (flakes, powder, salt) — a substitute for fresh onion

Orange Peel — baked goods, pork, game birds, garnish, marinade

Parsley (dried) — sauces, stuffing, marinades, soups, hot vegetables

(For items not listed here, see SPICES or specific heading. See also MAIL ORDER HERBS.)

HONEY — Store small amounts of honey in your dry pantry for pouring and dripping use. Honey can mold if left too long in the dry pantry; refrigeration is best for long term storage. If, during cold storage, the honey crystallizes, set the container in a pan of medium-hot water to allow it to liquify. Use spray-on vegetable oil in the measuring spoon or cup before pouring or measuring honey so that it will release better. If you substitute honey for half the sugar in recipes, use half honey and half sugar, then reduce liquids in the recipe by one quarter. If you are using all honey in the recipe instead of sugar, reduce the liquids called for by half. Doughs and cakes made with honey should be cooked at a slightly lower temperature.

HORS D'OEUVRES — Puff pastry canapés can be frozen, unfilled, for weeks until needed, but they must be served immediately after filling. Sandwich canapés can be prepared and stored in the refrigerator for twelve to twenty-four hours, covered with a damp paper towel, then plastic. Other canapés also have a short storage life, due to exposure to elements and varied perishability of ingredients.

HYDRATOR TUB — This humidity-controlled drawer of the refrigerator prevents over or under moisturization of vegetables and fruits which have been placed there. If you do not have a hydrator tub, use plastic bags to wrap vegetables which require humidity control, and add a paper towel or two to absorb any condensating liquids within the bag.

### -I-

ICE CREAM — Ice cream can be stored in the freezer for one month or until the date on the package indicates perishability. Never eat thawed and refrozen ice cream, because there are toxins which can develop in thawing and refreezing.

ICE CUBE TRAY — Use your ice cube tray to freeze liquids in small portions for future use. The average ice cube is equal to approximately 3 tablespoons of liquid. Any liquid to be frozen must be boiled first if you do not want air bubbles in the final cubes. Freeze leftover tea or coffee for using in iced tea and iced coffee without diluting the beverage.

ICING — You can store icing in the refrigerator or freezer until the end of the term of the most perishable ingredient present. For example, butter cream frosting contains butter, which has a storage life of two to three weeks in the refrigerator and two months in the freezer. Confectioner's sugar glaze, on the other hand, contains powdered sugar and water, so freezing will keep it safely, if tightly sealed, for six to twelve months. You must heat it after thawing, however, to liquify the frosting before using.

INFUSING (herbs and liquids) — To enhance the flavors of herbs you add or use in cooking, an infusion (or extract) can be made. Add to 1 cup wine (red or white), juice (fruit or vegetable), stock or water, 1 teaspoon of the chosen herb or 1/2 teaspoon each of two desired herbs. Simmer in a heavy saucepan for 10 minutes, then add 1 teaspoon butter; simmer an additional 5 minutes. Use as needed or place in a bottle or jar and store in the refrigerator.

ITALIAN SEASONING — Make your own Italian seasoning to use in recipes and sprinkle on vegetables: combine 3 tablespoons each of dried basil, oregano, and rosemary; add 1 or 2 teaspoons each garlic powder and dried thyme leaves. This recipe makes approximately 1/2 cup. Place it in an airtight container in the dry pantry for as long as six months. See also SPICES AND SPICED SEASONINGS.

ITALIAN SYRUPS — Flavored syrups used in preparing cream drinks such as latte's and cappucino, as well as in desserts. See Chapter 6, "Dessert Pantry," and Chapter 9, "Larder of Extracts, Liqueurs and Spirits."

## -J-

JAM — See JELLIES.

JARS — Using glass jars — either mason or recycled

condiment jars — is an efficient and attractive method of storing foods (except for those foods which must be stored in darkness) on your dry pantry shelf or in cold storage. Glass jars are simple to sterilize — simply place them in boiling water — and they make finding the item you have stored easier.

JELLIES (and jams) — Vacuum sealed jellies and jams can be stored for years on the dry pantry shelf. You can make quick fruit sauces with jams and jellies in several different ways: add equal portions of jelly solids to liqueurs; add fruit jams to whipped cream to taste; make a thin white sauce with water and tapioca flour (see THICKENERS) and add jam or jelly to flavor and color the sauce. Use for garnishing such desserts as cakes, puddings and ice cream.

JERUSALEM ARTICHOKES — This nutty flavored tuber should be stored like potatoes, in a cool, dark place.

JICAMA — Store it in the hydrator tub of the refrigerator for as long as two weeks.

JUNIPER BERRIES — See HERBAL SEASONINGS AND SEEDS.

### -K-

KALE — This spinach-like green should be stored in the hydrator tub with paper toweling wrapped closely to absorb moisture droplets; it will keep well for one or two weeks. Sauté kale in its own juices with a little bacon fat to cut the bitterness.

KETCHUP — Ketchup will store in the dry pantry for one to three years; if it begins to darken, spoilage may occur. Once it has been opened, keep it in the refrigerator to retain moisture; use within one year.

KIDNEYS (beef, veal) — Store fresh kidneys in the refrigerator for no more than one week. This product may be frozen for three months.

KIDNEYS (poultry) — Use fresh poultry kidneys within two days (unless you freeze them); poultry products have a high perishability factor. In the freezer, reserve kidneys which came with whole poultry until you have enough for an entire meal; freezer life is three months.

KOHLRABI — This leafy member of the cabbage family can be stored for two weeks in the refrigerator, one year in the freezer.

## -L-

LABELS — Keep an adequate supply of labels or freezer tape on hand for labeling foods going into the freezer or pantry. Note the name of the product, date and portion amount (if necessary). Learn to read the labels on all packaged foods which you may purchase. Look for the actual cost per ounce, pound, gram or liter; also notice any perishability date on the package. Plastic adhesive tape often works better than precut labels. You can write on the tape, and the adhesion will withstand everything from the freezer to the dishwasher.

LAMB — Lamb actually improves in flavor if you allow the meat to age a few days in the refrigerator before cooking, but the meat should not be stored there for more than four or five days. When purchasing lamb chops, always buy them thick-cut; their freezer life is four or five months. You can keep lamb roast and leg of lamb in the freezer for a year. Rub lemon juice all over a leg of lamb prior to cooking; the juice acts as a natural tenderizer and adds to the final flavor. Especially excellent herbs and seasonings for lamb are caraway and rosemary; garlic is essential.

LARDING — Rubbing salt pork or using larding strips woven into lean meats will add flavor and juice. Larding strips must be refrigerated; salt pork can be frozen for four months.

LEEKS — Store leeks in the hydrator tub of your refrigerator for as long as two weeks. Leeks may be substituted for onions in many recipes for a decisive taste difference. Sautéed leek is excellent by itself or with a vegetable sauce.

LEFTOVERS (planovers) — If you know you have prepared more than your family or guests will consume, separate out the extras immediately after cooking. Main dish meats, poultry and casseroles should be put in smaller containers (if you haven't already prepared them that way) or placed on TV dinner-style trays or plastic dishes and sealed. Set them directly into the storage of choice. Quick freezing planovers — straight from the oven (placed in cool containers) — ensures ideal quality of the foods for serving at another time. Reheating planovers is as simple as putting them, frozen, in a warm oven or microwave. Some frozen foods such as herbs, fresh ginger, vegetables, pastas, rice and crumb toppings are best used unthawed; just add them to recipes or bring to a boil and serve. The refrigerator life of pre-cooked foods is short, so check the ingredient with the shortest safe storage time; let that be your guide.

For freezer times, prepared foods are best used within a month, but certain foods, such as lasagna, vegetables, and rice or noodle casseroles can be frozen safely for four months. Pre-cooked meats should be reheated carefully. It is best to add them, cold or frozen, to the hot sauce or dish, allowing the warm food to heat the meats thoroughly; this prevents toughening of the meat or poultry. Poultry casseroles and bread stuffings are highly perishable; make certain that they are reheated directly from the freezer. Planned-over rice or pasta are excellent when added to fresh or frozen soups. Residual wine can be added to vinegar for your own supply of wine vinegar. Crumble and freeze baked goods — such as cookies and cakes — for a resource of dessert toppings to have on hand.

LEGUMES — Fresh legumes, such as snap beans, lima beans, peas and snow peas can be stored safely in the hydrator tub of your refrigerator for two weeks, but blanching and freezing is a more successful storing method. Enzymatic processes within the fresh legume can spoil flavor as well as texture; that's why blanching and freezing is a better method of storage. Dried legumes, such as lentils, split and yellow peas, garbanzos, navy and assorted dried beans can be safely stored on the dry pantry shelf for a year; discoloration means deterioration. Once cooked, dried legumes will store in the refrigerator for eight to ten days, depending on the meats involved in the cooking process; the legume dish can be frozen successfully for as long as six months. Leftover ham bones and purchased ham hocks are the basis of every excellent dried legume stew or soup. See HAM HOCKS.

LEMON — Fresh lemons store well in the refrigerator for as long as two weeks. You can freeze the rind of lemons (zest) for six to nine months; juice will keep in the freezer for a year. Before squeezing the fruit, grate the rind off. Squeeze and strain lemon juice in ice cube trays for quick use while cooking. One full cube equals approximately the juice of one lemon. Lemons can be substituted for limes. Lemons are easily squeezed if you roll the uncut lemon under the palm of your hand, with slight pressure, on a board or counter. You need not strain the juice for use in cakes, pies, cookies, or breads; simply remove the seeds. To extract just a few drops of lemon juice, prick the lemon with a fork or chop stick, then squeeze out the juice; the lemon can be put back into the refrigerator, none the worse for wear. Add 1 teaspoon lemon juice to 3 tablespoons softened butter and 1 teaspoon fresh chopped parsley to make lemon butter garnish for fish and seafood; allow it to harden in the refrigerator or freezer, then make balls or slices. Lemon juice in water retards the browning of fresh cut apples, pears, and vegetables such as cauliflower and potatoes. Three to four tablespoons of lemon juice is equal to the juice of one lemon.

LEMON GRASS (citronella) — Used as a main flavoring ingredient in Oriental dishes, the base of the stalk is most commonly chopped (as in green onions). You can substitute 1/2 grated lemon peel (zest) for 1 stalk lemon grass.

LEMON PEPPER — See SPICES.

LEMON THYME — See HERBS.

LEMON VERBENA — See HERBS.

LETTUCE - See SALAD GREENS.

LIGONBERRIES — Swedish cranberries, uncultivated

LIMA BEANS — See BEANS.

LIMES — Limes can be stored and used as lemons; see LEMONS. Limes are juicier if allowed to age. Young limes are dark green; as they age, they turn pale green, then yellow.

LIVER — In whole form or sliced, liver can be stored, tightly sealed, in your refrigerator for three days. Frozen, liver is storable for a year, but using it within three or four months is most ideal. Liver paté can be stored in your refrigerator for two weeks if it is covered in a layer of fat. However, freezing it for later use is better than allowing it to sit in the refrigerator, for its strong aroma may permeate other foods.

LOBSTER — See also SHELLFISH. Reserve the shell of lobster to cut into small pieces; sautéed or boiled in the recipe's liquids, the shell adds great flavor to the finished dish or sauce.

LOBSTER SEASONING — Use this in boiling liquids for all fresh cooked seafoods to bring out meat flavors. Purchase ready made or use: 2 bay leaves, 8 whole black peppercorns, 1 tablespoon parsley, 1/4 teaspoon fennel seeds, and 1/2 cup onion to 8 cups of water. Bring all to a boil and add lobster or other seafood.

LOVAGE — See HERBS.

## -M-

MACADAMIA NUTS — See NUTS.

MACE — See SPICES.

MACAROONS — Keep macaroons, wrapped individually if possible, in the dry pantry. Do not freeze. Keep leftover crumbs in a tightly sealed jar. When needed, toast the crumbs in a 200° F oven for 40 to 45 minutes or until they begin to crumble; use the fine crumbs in making pie crusts and frostings or with ice cream as a garnish.

MACARONI — See PASTA.

MADEIRA — Madeira is like port; it is used in cooking desserts and meat sauces. Keep it in the dry pantry indefinitely.

MAIL ORDER HERBS — You can order herbs from these catalogs if you have no resource for them available; call HERBAL EFFECT, 1-408-375-6855 or FOX HILL FARMS 1-517-531-3179 for catalogs.

MANGOES — Store mangoes in the dry pantry until ripe (when the peel is red-orange). You may freeze this fruit in pureé form for as long as two years; using the product within six to twelve months is ideal.

MANZANILLA — Dry sherry used in meat cookery.

MAPLE SYRUP — See also SYRUP. Make your own maple syrup to use in recipes as well as for pouring over pancakes, waffles and crêpes. In a medium sauce pan bring 1 cup water to boil; add 2 cups granulated (vanilla) sugar, stirring until completely dissolved, but not boiling. Mix in 1 teaspoon pure maple extract; store in bottles on a shelf of the dry pantry.

MARASCHINO CHERRIES — These can be stored in the dry pantry until opening. After being opened, they can be refrigerated for a year.

MARGARINE — This can be stored in the refrigerator for two to four weeks. For longer storage, margarine can be frozen for six months. Since this product has no animal fats or polyunsaturates, try using half margarine and half butter combinations in your recipes (instead of all butter). You'll retain the rich butter flavor and gain the benefits of margarine's lower cholesterol level, as well as less cost.

MARIGOLDS — See HERBS.

MARINADES — Purchased marinades can sit on the dry pantry shelf indefinitely, if unopened. Marinades you've used can be reused over and over by simply straining and sealing tightly in a jar or container; this will keep in the refrigerator for as long as three weeks. Because of the oil content in most marinades, separation will occur in freezing; in addition, there will be a flavor loss of herbs and spices inherent to the marinade. Therefore freezing is not recommended, though it can be done.

MARINARA SAUCE — Here's a recipe for preparing your own fresh marinara: heat 1/2 cup olive oil in a heavy saucepan and add 3 large onions (chopped) and 2 cloves garlic (minced); sauté for 5 minutes; add 6 cups tomatoes (seeded and diced), 1/2 teaspoon dried oregano, 1 tablespoon dried parsley, 1/2 teaspoon dried basil and 1/2 teaspoon sugar. Simmer, covered, and stir occasionally for an hour. Add salt and pepper to taste. Prepare ahead of time and keep it on hand; pour this over such foods as chicken, cheeses and pasta, as desired. It can be frozen in half portions for later use.

MARJORAM — See HERBS.

MARMALADE GLAZE — For dressing up pork chops, chicken, and ham, make your own marmalade glaze; into a small saucepan combine 1/2 cup orange juice, 1/2 cup orange marmalade and 1 tablespoon honey. Bring to a boil and immediately turn down the heat; simmer for approximately 15 minutes or until thick. Refrigerate the glaze until it is needed.

MARSALA — This Italian cooking wine can be stored in the dry pantry until it is opened. Follow directions on the bottle or jar with regard to refrigeration after opening.

MARSHMALLOWS — Marshmallows will store on a dry pantry shelf for six to eight weeks. Ideally, marshmallows freeze very well, and you won't run the risk of their drying out. They can be frozen for six to twelve months. Keep a supply of both mini and regular marshmallows for salads and cooking. To cut marshmallows, first dip scissors in water.

MASHED POTATOES — Prepared mashed potatoes can be stored in the refrigerator for one week, though freezing in small (1 cup) portions — for as long as six months — is best for utilizing extras. Use frozen mashed potatoes to extend creamed soups and chowders. To keep the potatoes white, add 1/2 cup sour cream and 1 tablespoon lemon juice per 10 potatoes when mashing.

MATZO FLOUR — Whole wheat flour milled according to kosher requirements. Store in dry pantry, sealed, for as long as 1 year. See also Unleavened Breads.

MAYONNAISE — Unopened, store-bought mayonnaise has an indefinite shelf life. Once opened, prepared mayonnaise can be stored in the refrigerator for three to six months before retrograding or drying out occurs. Freshly made mayonnaise must be used quickly, since the emulsion is not as stable as store-bought; the flavor of homemade, however, is superior. Make up your own in small portions, being sure to use all of it in two to five days. Do not freeze any mayonnaise.

MEASURES — See "Appendix: Pantry Charts and Tables."

MEAT EXTENDERS — Ground meat extenders include rice, certain pasta, nonfat dry milk powder, bread crumbs, raw grated potatoes, instant potato flakes, potato chips (ground) and ground leftover vegetables.

MEAT GLAZE — See GLAZE.

MEAT LOAF — Cooked, ground meat dishes can be stored in the refrigerator for three days. Freezing is best for storage longer than two days; the loaf can be frozen for as long as three months without deterioration. Use grated raw potatoes as a filler in meat loaf preparation. This helps bind the meats together as well as retaining moisture content. Try using ground turkey the next time you make a meat loaf; add a little sage and poultry seasoning to the mix, and you'll have a tasty, lower calorie, lower cholesterol entrée.

MEATS — Large cuts of meat can be safely stored in the refrigerator for three to five days. Ground meats are highly perishable and should not sit unused in the refrigerator for more than two or three days. Cured meats can be stored in the refrigerator for a week. For details on freezer life of specific meat, refer to its category in this resource guide. In general, beef roasts, lamb roasts and steaks can be frozen for eight to twelve months; pork and veal roasts for four to eight months; pork and lamb chops and steaks for three to four months; ground meats for two to three months; cured meats for one month; cooked meats for two or three months. Thaw frozen meats in the bottom of your refrigerator for six to eight hours. Use any thawed meats within two days; thaw in the refrigerator and remove the meat only within one hour of the beginning of cooking time to allow large cuts of meat to achieve room temperature before roasting. When preparing steaks and chops for freezing, wrap them with waxed paper between the cuts before adding the exterior wrap. Freeze ground meat in flat slabs to allow the cold temperature to evenly penetrate the meat; freeze ground meat patties with waxed paper dividers.

MELONS — Melons store well in the refrigerator for two weeks; one week is the optimum time. Melon sections can be frozen, but the texture will be slightly affected. Ripe melons can give off a delightfully sweet smell, but you may wish to wrap cut melons to keep the odor from permeating other foods in your refrigerator.

MERINGUES — You can store desserts with meringue and meringue topping in the refrigerator for three to five days; do not freeze.

MESCLUN — French name for a mixture of baby salad greens.

METRICS — See temperature chart in "Appendix: Pantry Charts and Tables." General metric conversions for cooking are: 1 oz. = 28 gms.; 1 c. = 1/4 liter; 1 pt. = 1/2 liter; 1 qt. = .946 liter; 1 lb. = 450 gms.; 2.2 lbs. = 1 kilogram.

MILK — Store fresh milk in the refrigerator for five to seven days. Whole containers of milk can be frozen for as long as six months; allow it to thaw in the refrigerator for two days before using. You can make your own 2% milk by purchasing whole (4% milkfat) and adding to it an equal portion of prepared nonfat dry milk. Use nonfat dry milk as much as you can in cooking and baking — for convenience as well as low cholesterol benefits. You can use canned skim milk as a low calorie and low cholesterol substitute for cream; another substitute for cream is scalded regular milk which is strained before use in coffee and beverages. Evaporated milk is an excellent substitute for whole milk in cooking; use equal parts water and evaporated milk. You can use full strength evaporated milk as a substitute for cream. To make your own sour cream, add 1 tablespoon vinegar per 1 cup of undiluted evaporated milk, and allow to stand 5 minutes. You can extend purchased buttermilk from 1 quart to 4 quarts by combining 1 quart buttermilk and 3 quarts lukewarm skimmed milk, adding 1/4 teaspoon salt and mixing well. Allow this to stand at room temperature for one day, covered, then refrigerate. You can substitute sweet milk (whole or lowfat) for buttermilk in cooking, by adding 2 teaspoons either vinegar or lemon juice to 1 scant cup milk; allow to sit 5 minutes at room temperature before using. You can substitute buttermilk for sour milk in any recipe. Make homemade cakes and cookies more tender by substituting sour milk or buttermilk for the sweet milk called for in the recipe; add 1/2 to 1 teaspoon baking soda to the dry ingredients to counter-balance acidic action; this gives desserts extra delicacy.

MIREPOIX — This custom-made blend of vegetables and seasonings is sautéed and used to flavor other dishes such as casseroles, meats, poultry, seafoods, gravies and sauces. These allow you to cut down on salt and fats which are normally used to season bland foods. Prepare and store mirepoix in the refrigerator for as long as two weeks or freeze it in an ice cube tray (giving you access to 3 tablespoon portions) and keep the cubes in a freezer bag for as long as one year. Basic mirepoix is made of: 1 cup celery and 1 cup onion, both chopped fine; 1 tablespoon butter (or nut oil), 2 cloves garlic (crushed), 1 to 2 teaspoons of crushed herbs of choice such as: oregano, parsley, basil, thyme, marjoram and savory. Add herbs after sautéing vegetables in butter or oil for 5 minutes; simmer 2 or 3 more minutes. Remove mirepoix to a bowl and deglaze pan with 1 tablespoon dry sherry or vermouth. Add to mirepoix, mix and store.

MISO PASTE — After opening, store this soybean paste in the refrigerator pantry.

MOLASSES — Store molasses on a dry pantry shelf, optimally, for one year. You can make a substitute for brown sugar with white sugar and molasses. Measure 1 cup less 2 tablespoons white sugar and add 1/4 cup molasses; mix and allow to stand for one hour.

MOLLUSKS — See SHELLFISH.

MSG — See SPICES AND SPICED SEASONINGS.

MUFFINS — Store muffins in an airtight bag in the dry pantry for 3 to 5 days. Freeze muffins for as long as four months. Reheat them directly from being frozen. Try using leftover muffins as a hollowed out cup for fruits and sauces. To make muffins easily, prepare a large batch of muffin base-mix and store it in dry pantry, tightly sealed, for as long as six months. Then, when you want to make a quick batch, use this base mix. In a large bowl combine 10 cups all-purpose flour, 1 1/2 cups sugar, 1/3 cup baking powder, 1 tablespoon salt; mix well. With a pastry blender, stir in 2 1/2 to 3 cups shortening and combine until mixture resembles coarse crumbs. Place in an airtight container. When you are ready to make muffins, take out 2 1/2 cups mix, add 1 beaten egg, 2/3 cup milk and 1 cup of your favorite berries or puréed fruit. Stir just until blended, adding more milk as needed to create a thick, lumpy batter. Spoon into muffin cups, 3/4 full, and bake at 400° F for 20 minutes.

MUSHROOMS - Unwashed mushrooms will keep for five to seven days in the refrigerator, in a brown paper bag. You can freeze them for six to twelve months; wash them and leave whole or slice, then place in them in a freezer bag. Use them in cooking without defrosting. You can dry your own mushrooms by stringing them popcorn-style and hanging them for two or three days. When they are thoroughly dry, place them in containers and store them in the dry pantry for as long as six months. Rehydrate dried mushrooms by soaking them in very warm water for one hour; use the soaking liquids in your recipe. Prepared mushrooms (*duxelles*) will keep in the perishables pantry for three to five days.

MUSSELS — See SHELLFISH.

MUSTARD — See HERBS AND SEEDS. As a condiment, prepared mustard can be refrigerated after opening for six to twelve months. Do not freeze.

MUTTON — See MEATS for storage information. Though mutton is a tougher and gamier meat than lamb, it is often prepared and served in the same manner. After removing *all* surface fat, rub lemon over the entire surface of the mutton before roasting. The lemon gives added flavor and acts as a tenderizer.

### -N-

NASTURTIUMS — Flowerets used in salads, as a garnish. Store them, unwashed, in a plastic bag in the refrigerator for as long as one week. They do not freeze well. See HERBAL SEASONINGS AND SEEDS.

NECTARINES — Store nectarines, unwashed, in the refrigerator for as long as two weeks.

NEW POTATOES — Store new potatoes in the hydrator tub of the refrigerator for as long as two weeks. For ideal texture, always cook new potatoes in rapidly boiling salted water. (Winter potatoes should be cooked by adding them to cold salted water and then brought to a boil.)

NONFAT DRY MILK — When this is well sealed, it will store in the dry pantry for one or two years. See MILK for other hints and suggestions.

NUTMEG — See SPICES.

NUTS — Store nuts still in the shell in the dry pantry for no longer than one month. Keep opened cans and jars, tightly sealed, in the refrigerator. Nuts — either in shell or removed from shell — can be frozen indefinitely; however, there is a potential for the natural oils to dry out, so freezing for longer than two years is not recommended. You do not need to thaw nut meats; simply chop and use them frozen. Coat nut meats with flour before putting them in batters and other baked dishes; this prevents the nuts from sinking to the bottom while cooking.

## Commonly Used Nuts

Almonds — available in shell, whole unshelled, blanched and unblanched, sliced, slivered, whole roasted, and paste form

Brazil nuts — available whole, in shell and un-shelled, sliced

Cashews — actually a seed that has no shell; available plain, salted and in bits

Chestnuts — sold in the shell, canned, dried; fresh chestnuts must be used within three months.

Coconuts — Available whole, coconuts can be stored in the dry pantry for as long as six months. Once they have been opened, they should be refrigerated and used within a week.

Filberts — cultivated hazelnuts

Hazelnuts — available shelled, unshelled and in bits

Macadamia — available shelled whole and in bits

Peanuts — available in shell, unshelled, salted or unsalted and dry roasted

Pecans — sold in shell, shelled, roasted, dry roasted, salted, and plain

Pinenuts (pignolias) — available raw or toasted

See also main heading in "Resource Guide."

Pistachios — available in shell (red or natural pale green), shelled, salted, or plain

Walnuts — available in shell, shelled, in pieces

### *-O-*

OATS — Oats may be stored, tightly sealed, in the dry pantry for six to twelve months.

OILS — Most oils, especially nut oils, store best in a dark cupboard at approximately room temperature. Vegetable oils such as olive oils can go rancid if stored too long, so you may prefer to refrigerate them. Some oils cloud up during refrigeration, but the oil will clear up after being brought back to room temperature. Dry pantry storage of most oils is six to twelve months.

OKRA — This mucilaginous vegetable may be stored, unwashed, in the refrigerator for as long as two weeks. Don't purchase okra with a length exceeding 3 inches. You can use okra as a natural thickener to soups, stews and gumbo.

OLIVADA — Olive paste is used in regional Italian cooking. To make your own olivada, purée pitted, black brine-cured olives (kalamata for example) in a food processor. A half cup of olives will make 1/3 cup olivada. Store it in the refrigerator pantry.

OLIVE OIL — Pale olive oils are predominantly the last pressing; the oil turns from darker green to golden with the first, second, and third pressing. Usually, the richer the color, the richer the flavor, although there are oils which are pale golden yellow that are quite rich. Olive oils will endure a shelf life of three to six months when stored in dark bottles or dark cupboards; you may refrigerate little-used oils to ensure their freshness.

OLIVES — Olives, unopened, have an enduring shelf life; refrigeration is recommended after opening.

OLOROSO — sweet sherry used in making desserts

OMELETS — An excellent entrée to make, using leftover meats and vegetables from your refrigerator. Leftover omelets should be consumed within two days.

ONIONS — Store all onions — with the exception of leeks and scallions, which require refrigeration — in a cool (not cold), dry, preferably dark place. Do not enclose them in plastic bags, for unpeeled, uncut onions need recirculating air. After they've been peeled and/or cut, store them in a plastic bag or sealed container for no longer than seven days in the refrigerator. White onions are more perishable than yellow or red. Most raw onions have a shelf life of two or three weeks. Do not purchase any onions with green sprouts, which are an indication of spoilage. Scallions can be kept fresh by removing the outer layers which become brown during storage. You can freeze peeled, chopped onions — for later use in cooking — for as long as six months. To use a portion of a large onion and retain the freshness of the unused part, chop off the needed amount, unpeeled, and cover the cut end with plastic; the peel of the onion is its natural preservative. Room temperature onions weep less than cold ones when being chopped. Most dishes to which you are adding onions are enhanced if you sauté the onions in butter or oil first. You can make an excellent low calorie sauce for meats and vegetables by boiling onions (1 cup chopped onions to 1 cup liquid) in either stock or water until transparent; purée them, along with the juices. Flavor this base with your favorite seasonings and use it as either a sauce or a base for soup or dressings. See also MIREPOIX.

ORANGE FLAVORED WATER — Store this in the dry pantry; keep tightly sealed.

ORANGES — You may keep oranges in the dry pantry for two or three weeks. Grate rind (zest) off exterior of washed oranges which you plan to juice; freeze the rind for as long as nine months for use in recipes and garnish. One half cup orange juice is equal to one medium orange. You can substitute orange juice for wine in cooking, especially for fish. For a lovely edible garnish, parboil juliennes of orange rind, then add to sauces or use for topping entrées.

OREGANO — See HERBS AND SPICES.

ORIENTAL NOODLE SOUP (ramen) — Keep assorted flavors handy for making quick, hot meals; simply add appropriate meat after preparing the noodles. They can also be used for crumbling into salads and other recipes.

OYSTER PLANT — See SALSIFY.

OYSTER SAUCE — This is an oriental condiment used as a seasoning; it is made up of reduced oyster juices and salt. Store in the perishable pantry for as long as one year.

OYSTERS — See MOLLUSKS.

### -P-

PALM SUGAR — This coarse brown sugar can be stored in the dry pantry. You can use regular brown sugar as a substitute.

PANADA — This thickening agent for soup and sauces can be made ahead and kept in the refrigerator for two to four weeks. A basic panada contains 1/4 cup flour to 2 tablespoons melted butter or oil; mix well over medium heat, then measure 8 tablespoons water or milk. Incorporate the liquid into the flour and butter until the mixture separates from the sides of the pan. Spread it on a butter dish or plate, and slice off portions as needed. Keep panada covered in the refrigerator and use it as a substitute for flour listed in recipes. Your foods will never taste floury when you use a panada.

PANCAKES — Leftover pancakes can be frozen, as crêpes, between sheets of waxed paper. Warm them from the frozen state on a cookie sheet at 350° F until heated through, approximately 10 minutes.

PAPAYA — Refrigerate unwashed papaya when ripe — the skin will be deep yellow to orange — for as long as two weeks. Candied papaya can be stored in the dry pantry for a year.

PAPRIKA — See SPICES.

PARSLEY — See HERBS AND HERB SEASONINGS.

PARMESAN — See CHEESE.

PARSNIPS — Refrigerate unwashed parsnips for as long as two or three weeks; use them as you would carrots, either alone or in soups and stews.

PASTA — *Fresh* pasta, ideally, should be cooked from room temperature. This means that if you make your own, it should be stored in a sealed container in your dry pantry. Egg pasta can be safely stored for two days this way; flour and oil pasta can be kept for two weeks. If you are unable to use your fresh pasta within this time, refrigerate it — or better, freeze it, for as long as six months. Dried, commercial pastas — such as spaghetti and macaroni — can be stored indefinitely in your dry pantry in a sealed container.

PASTRY DOUGH - You may refrigerate pastry dough, wrapped tightly in plastic, for three or four days. It can be frozen for as long as six months. Baked pastry crusts, wrapped airtight in their tins, can be frozen for a year.

PATÉ — Refrigerate unused paté for as long as three days. You can freeze it for three months.

PATÉ A CHOUX — Specialty dough used for making éclairs, cream puffs and filled hors d'oeuvres.

PATTY SHELLS — You can make patty shells from puff pastry ahead of time, then freeze them between layers of wax paper in an airtight container. They will keep for four months. Fresh-baked patty shells will keep crisp for three or four days in your dry pantry, if they're wrapped as indicated above; do not refrigerate.

PEACHES — Refrigerate unwashed peaches for as long as three weeks, but use them immediately if they become soft to the touch. Reserve juices from canned peaches, either to add to fruit juice or to use as a base for a dessert sauce.

PEANUT BUTTER — Store opened peanut butter in the dry pantry for as long as six months. Refrigerate for longer storage.

PEANUTS — See NUTS.

PEARS — Store pears at room temperature for as long as two weeks. Reserve juices of canned pears to add to fruit juice or to use as a base for a dessert sauce.

PEAS — Fresh peas (in pod) can be stored in the refrigerator, optimally, for one week. For longer storage — as long as one year — it is best to de-pod them, blanche and freeze, since the starches inherent in fresh peas can alter their taste and texture over prolonged storage. Steam or sauté peas, just to al denté, in chicken stock; reserve liquids for your next soup or stew.

PECANS — See NUTS.

PECTIN — Preserving and thickening agent for fruits and berries

PEPPER — See SPICES.

PEPPERS (capsicum family) — Refrigerate peppers no longer than two weeks. Freezing for as long as four months is fine for chopped or diced peppers which are to be used in future dishes — for color as well as flavor. However, whole or sliced peppers lose texture and body in freezing because of their high moisture content; they're unattractive in whole form after thawing. Always use rubber gloves when handling peppers to avoid burning skin and eyes.

PERISHABLES PANTRY — Your refrigerator!

PERSIAN MELONS — Refrigerate unwashed melons for as long as two weeks.

PERSIMMONS — Store persimmons at room temperature until fully ripe, then refrigerate for no longer than two weeks.

PESTO — This is a prepared combination of pureed herbs (predominantly basil) and oil, with garlic, Parmesan cheese and pine nuts; it is used as a spread or sauce. Store it in the perishables pantry, no longer than two weeks, or freeze with a layer of oil over surface, as long as six months.

PICKLED LEMONS — These will keep in the dry pantry for a year.

PICKLES — Once opened, pickles must be refrigerated, although they maintain a relatively long storage life — one or two years.

PIE CRUST — See PASTRY.

PIES — Most pies can be stored in the refrigerator for one week, though meringue and custard pies should be consumed within three days. You can successfully store frozen unbaked fruit pies for three to six months; bake them directly from frozen state. Freeze *baked* fruit pies after cooling by placing paper plates over the tops and wrapping tightly. Let pre-baked frozen pies thaw in a moderate oven for 20 or 30 minutes, or let them stand at room temperature for three or four hours. Chiffon pies freeze well for as long as three months, but never freeze any custard or egg based pies; the egg emulsions are unstable. You should add 1/3 more thickening agent to fruit pies which you plan to freeze, in order to cut down on the sogginess which freezing can create. Also, you might sprinkle the bottom of pie crusts you plan to freeze with fine bread crumbs or leftover cookie or cake crumbs to prevent crusts from becoming soggy.

PIMENTO (capsicum family) — See PEPPERS.

PINEAPPLE — Uncut pineapples store best at room temperature. Cut pineapple must be tightly sealed for storage in the refrigerator, for no longer than five days. Pineapple chunks and slices do not freeze well; you can, however, freeze juice and pulp for as long as six months.

PINE NUTS (pignolias) — See NUTS for storage information. To make salted pine nuts for snacking, mix 1 cup pine nuts with 2 teaspoons unsalted, melted butter; add 1 teaspoon ground salt or a mixture of crushed herbs; bake on a cookie sheet for 15 minutes at 300°, stirring every 5 minutes. Cool and serve.

PLASTIC CONTAINERS — Maintain a supply of containers and discard any that have inadequate seals. Remove any stains (and odors) on plastic with water and baking soda, as a scouring medium.

PLUMS — Store fresh plums, unwashed, in the refrigerator. You can freeze uncooked, pitted plums; for best flavor, however, stew them prior to freezing.

POLENTA — You can store these finely milled corngrains in the dry pantry for a year.

POMEGRANATES — Store pomegranates at room temperature. Ripe pomegranate seeds make a colorful juice or sauce base. Place peeled fruit in a food mill or blender and liquify; strain and freeze the juice for use in punches, gelatins, aspics, and as a base for dessert sauces.

POPCORN — Popcorn has a shelf life of two years, though use before this time is suggested. Store it in the dry pantry. If you wash popcorn and drain it before popping, the kernels will pop more easily.

POPOVERS — Store fresh-baked popovers, wrapped airtight, in the dry pantry for no longer than three days. They are best stored frozen; when needed, simply place the frozen popovers in foil and bake them for 5 minutes at 425° F.

PORK — Store fresh cuts of pork for no longer than three days in your refrigerator; for assured quality in storing pork, freeze for as long as eight months for roasts and four months for chops and steaks. Ground pork which is frozen should be stored no longer than three months.

POTATO CHIPS — Stored in the dry pantry, potato chips will last in a sealed container as long as two weeks after they've been removed from the original bag. You *can* freeze potato chips. Utilize leftover chips as ground crumbs for breading meats, in croquettes, and as a crunchy topping for vegetable dishes.

POTATO SALAD — Because of the mayonnaise and egg combination in potato salad, it can be stored no longer than three to five days in the refrigerator.

POTATO STARCH (flour) — Use 2/3 teaspoon of this thickening agent to substitute for 2 teaspoons flour or 1 teaspoon cornstarch in a recipe for thickening a sauce. Potato starch will not make the sauce opaque.

POTATO WATER — After boiling potatoes, strain the water carefully and reserve it for use in soups; it is a very nutritious liquid. You can also use potato water as liquid needed in yeast doughs and breads, for a finer textured baked product. Boil liquids down in order to reduce them for easy storage.

POTATOES (See also NEW POTATOES.) — The best storage for potatoes is in a dark, cool room or in a brown bag with holes punched in it — to allow air to circulate. If storing your potatoes this way allows *eyes* to develop, you aren't using them quickly enough; purchase smaller quantities in your next marketing plan. You can store new potatoes in the refrigerator, but prolonged storage will allow conversion of the starches in your potatoes to sugars; the potatoes will break down in texture, as well as flavor. Fresh (and even cooked) potatoes do not freeze well; however, leftover *mashed* potatoes can be frozen and used in recipes calling for extenders, such as soups, stews and ground meat dishes. You can rebake a leftover baked potato by dipping it in water and putting it in a 350° F oven for 20 minutes. Use extra mashed potatoes as a garnish; pipe them through a pastry tube with a decorative tip over casseroles and meats. Brown them lightly in the oven before serving. Use grated raw potatoes to help bind hamburger patties, act as a nutritious extender for meat loaves, reduce saltiness, and thicken soups and stews. To cook winter potatoes, it is best to place them in cold, salted water, then bring to a boil.

POULTRY — Generally, fresh poultry is best used immediately after purchasing, due to the high incidence of salmonella. If storage is necessary, poultry, tightly covered, can be refrigerated no longer than three days. Freezing is a better means of storage for poultry; the smaller the item, the shorter the freezing time. As a rule, Cornish hens, turkeys, geese, whole chickens and roasters can be effectively stored in the freezer for as long as six months to a year, depending on the size. Cooked poultry storage times are much shorter than fresh: two to three months. Cut up chickens, pieces, and boned breasts, when stored before cooking, are best used within one to three months; this prevents freezer burn from drying out the meats. The best way to store leftover poultry is to remove all meat from bones, cover it with poultry gravy or stock, then freeze. Do not freeze any stuffed poultry.

POUND CAKE — Store pound cake, well wrapped, in the refrigerator for one or two weeks. This freezes well, though at less duration than other cakes because of its egg content. Recommended freezer duration is three to six months.

PRALINE POWDER — This confectionery ingredient can be stored in the dry pantry for as long as one year, if it is tightly sealed. You can make your own praline powder for sprinkling on top of desserts or adding to recipes for added flavor. Use 2 cups sugar, 3 tablespoons lemon juice, 1 cup blanched almonds and 1 cup hazelnuts. Heat sugar and lemon juice, stirring over medium heat until the syrup is golden. Add nuts, stir, then pour mixture into a jelly roll pan or on a marble slab, spreading it into as thin a layer as possible. Allow it to cool for approximately an hour, then break it into pieces. Place it in a food processor or blender and chop it into a fine powder, removing crushed praline as you process, placing it into separate containers as you continue chopping the larger pieces. (You can also crush it with a rolling pin.)

PREPARATION DAY — See COOKING DAY.

PRUNES — Store prunes in a plastic bag in the dry pantry as you would raisins, for as long as a year. Prunes can be frozen, but unless they are stewed, they lose flavor and moisture during freezing. It is best to stew prunes in prune juice in order to retain maximum flavor.

PUDDING — Most puddings will keep for a week, if they're stored in the refrigerator. Puddings cannot be frozen, because the emulsion retrogrades during the process of freezing and thawing.

PUFF PASTRY — This is the dough used for making patty shells, napoleons, and other types of gourmet foods. If you need to prepare a lot of pastries ahead of time, fresh-baked, unfilled pastries freeze extremely well. When you're ready to use them, place them in a 425° F oven for 3 to 5 minutes until warmed, then fill them as desired. (Available in freezer section of supermarket)

PUMPKIN — See SQUASH.

## -Q-

QUAIL — Treat, refrigerate and freeze quail in the same manner in which you handle small chickens and Cornish hens. Freezer life is no longer than three months, due to the small size of the bird.

QUATRE EPICES — See SPICES AND SPICED SEASONINGS.

QUENELLES — Store leftover quenelles according to the storage life of the most perishable item in the recipe, or no longer than three days in the refrigerator. You can freeze quenelles in sauce or gravy.

QUICHE — You can effectively refrigerate leftover quiche for as long as three days, although the crust can get soggy during that period. You can safely freeze prepared quiche (baked and cooled before placing in the freezer) for as long as three months.

QUICK BREADS — Popovers, muffins, waffles, pancakes, biscuits, shortbreads, scones and fruit/nut breads can be stored, well wrapped, in the dry pantry or refrigerator for a period ranging from two days to one week. It is better, however, to store these breads by freezing them, for as long as three months.

QUINCE — Store this tart fruit as you would oranges or lemons. Quince have a natural pectin inherent in the fruit; dejuiced, they can be used to make fruit syrups and liqueurs; its most common usage is in making marmalade.

QUINOA — You can use these little disk-shaped seeds (grains) in recipes as you would whole wheat berries or rice. Store tightly sealed in dry pantry for six months.

### -R-

RABBIT — Fresh rabbit can be refrigerated, well wrapped, for no longer than three to five days, due to its low fat content. Wrap it as you would chicken, then freeze whole rabbits six to twelve months and rabbit pieces for three months.

RADISH — Radishes can be kept, unwrapped, in the hydrator tub of the refrigerator for one or two weeks. It is better to remove the stems and place the radishes in water which is changed often; this method, however will keep them effectively in the refrigerator for no longer than five to seven days. Radishes do not freeze well.

RAISINS — Store raisins in sealed containers in the dry pantry for as long as one year. You can freeze them, but freezing affects the texture slightly. Rehydrate dried out raisins for use in cooking by blanching for 1 minute.

RASPBERRIES — See BERRIES.

RECIPE BOX — See CARD FILE.

RELISHES — Store unopened relishes and chutneys for as long as two years in the dry pantry. Once opened, these preparations still can be stored in the refrigerator for as long as a year.

RHUBARB — Refrigerate, unwrapped, for no longer than two weeks.

RICE — Uncooked rice, if sealed tightly, can be stored indefinitely in your dry pantry. You can keep a supply of cooked rice, sealed in an airtight container, in the refrigerator for several days. A better suggestion is to freeze your planned-over rice in 1 or 2 cup portions; it will keep for as long as six months. When you are ready to use refrigerated rice, pour boiling water over it and let it drain or add 2 tablespoons water to 2 cups rice, fluff and heat in the microwave. For frozen rice, put it in boiling water, then simmer for a few minutes before draining. These planned-over rices are perfect for adding to casseroles, combining with other foods (for a dish like Spanish rice), and using as meat and soup extenders.

RICE CAKES — Store rice cakes in the dry pantry. They can be frozen, also.

RICE FLOUR — Store rice flour, tightly sealed, in the dry pantry. To use as a substitute for wheat flours or other starches in food preparation, use slightly less rice flour than the proportion listed in the recipe, for example, 1 2/3 teaspoons rice flour will substitute for 2 teaspoons wheat flour.

RICE NOODLES — Also called rice sticks. Use rice noodles as a garnish or as an appetizer (by frying them in hot oil). Store them in the dry pantry.

RICOTTA — Store ricotta in the refrigerator for as long as two weeks or according to the date on the package. You can freeze it for as long as six months. As a base for fruit tarts, use ricotta combined with your favorite liqueur and sugar to taste. Substitution: Use whipped cottage cheese as a substitute for ricotta.

RIND — See ZEST.

ROASTS — For storage information, see specific meat. Frozen and thawed roasts require 1/3 less cooking time then fresh. Reserve bones from beef roasts for making stock.

ROLLS — Store rolls in the dry pantry for as long as five days; wrap them well to prevent crusts from drying out. Freeze rolls in a moisture-proof bag or container for as long as three to six months. Reheat rolls without drying out the crusts by dipping them in cool water and baking them at 250° F for 10 or 15 minutes; allow frozen rolls to defrost first.

ROSE WATER — Store rose water, tightly sealed, in the dry pantry.

ROSEMARY — See HERBS AND SEASONINGS.

ROUX (See also THICKENERS) — Store prepared roux — brown, yellow or white — in the refrigerator for as long as three months.

RUM — Keep a supply of dark and light rum on hand for use in cooking — especially for use in desserts. See Dessert Pantry.

RUTABAGA — See TURNIPS.

RYE FLOUR - Store small quantities in tightly sealed containers in the dry pantry for as long as three to six months; refrigerate or freeze for longer storage — as long as one year.

## -S-

SAFFRON — See SPICES.

SAGE — See HERBS AND HERBAL SEASONINGS.

SAGO STARCH — See THICKENERS.

SALAD DRESSING — Freshly made salad dressings should be used within a week, in order to fully take advantage of the fresh flavor. If you don't have time to make your own, bottled dressings are easily accessible and adequate; once they are opened, they can be stored for months in the refrigerator.

SALAD GREENS — If you keep fresh greens cool and dry, they will store well for one or two weeks. These include cabbages, endive, escarole, chicory, and lettuces such as butterhead, bibb, Boston, iceberg, romaine, imperial, and New York. Other leaf greens such as spinach, kale, collard greens, mustard greens, and red and green leaf lettuces perish more quickly, and should be used within a week. Herb greens such as parsley and watercress store best when their stems are placed in water in a covered container; with frequent water changes, they'll last as long as two weeks. Avoid immersing the tops. Do not wash greens prior to storing. Keep a paper towel in the container or plastic bag to absorb the moisture which can attach to leaves and increase perishability.

SALMON — See FISH for storage information. Smoked salmon has a longer refrigerator storage time then fresh. Wrapped well, smoked salmon will keep for as long as one month.

SALSIFY — Treat salsify shoots as you would spinach; use the roots as you would rutabaga or turnip.

SALT — Keep salt from moisture or humidity. Salt, as a condiment or seasoning, should be used sparingly on foods to be frozen, since saltiness diminishes during storage but the sodium presence does not. Do *not* double salt when doubling recipes. You can substitute sprinkled lemon juice or vinegar for salt in recipes and on vegetables.

SALTED DRIED SHRIMP — This ingredient is used in many Thai and other Oriental dishes. You can purchase it in small amounts and store it indefinitely in the perishables pantry.

SANDWICHES — Most sandwiches can be prepared in advance and stored up to twenty-four hours in the refrigerator. Meat and cheese sandwiches can be frozen and stored (do not freeze with greens) until 4 to 6 hours prior to consumption. Simply allow them to thaw at room temperature.

SAUCES — If you cannot use refrigerated, fresh made sauces within two days, you should freeze them; they'll keep for three months. Sauces made with mayonnaise, egg yolks and animal fats can retrograde after freezing and thawing. These sauces are fine once reblended, but consistency of the emulsion will be affected. Add 1/4 teaspoon powdered gelatin per 1 cup leftover sauce and stir well; this helps stabilize the sauce for freezing.

SAUERKRAUT — Keep sauerkraut in the refrigerator; freezing is not recommended.

SAUSAGES — Sausages stored in the refrigerator will keep no longer than three to five days, but they'll freeze well for three months. See also MEATS.

SCALLIONS — See ONIONS for storage information. Use the green stems of scallions to tie bundles of vegetables or meats for cooking.

SCALLOPS — See SHELLFISH.

SEAFOOD — Refrigerate all seafoods as quickly as possible. Some seafoods do best packed with crushed ice, with some of them keeping this way for three to five days. You can freeze seafoods for as long as six months. See also specific types, for more information.

SEASONING SALT — Make your own seasoning salt for use in cooking by adding to 1 cup salt: 1 tablespoon paprika, 2 teaspoons dry mustard, 2 teaspoons dried (crushed) oregano, 1 teaspoon garlic powder, and 1 teaspoon onion powder. Store in an airtight container.

SEASONINGS — See specific types, SPICES, and HERBS AND HERBAL SEASONINGS.

SELF RISING FLOUR - Store this flour in labeled, airtight containers for a long duration in the dry pantry. To make 1 cup of your own self rising flour, mix 1 cup sifted all-purpose flour with 1-1/2 teaspoons baking powder and 1/4 teaspoon salt.

SEMOLINA FLOUR — This hard grain flour is best stored, tightly sealed, in the refrigerator for twelve months. You can freeze it indefinitely.

SESAME OIL — Store in the dry pantry or dark cupboard in small quantities.

SESAME PASTE (Tahini) — This ground seed paste can be used as a substitute for peanut butter in many recipes, as well as making tahini. Store it in the refrigerator pantry after opening.

SESAME SEEDS — Store these in the dry pantry for as long as one year.

SHAD — See FISH.

SHALLOTS — This garlic-tasting member of the onion family can be stored in the dry pantry or, for more longevity, wrapped and placed in the refrigerator.

SHELLFISH — Scallops, mussels, clams, oysters, crab, shrimp, and lobster all perish quickly. They should be refrigerated, even kept on crushed ice, for their flavor and freshness can deteriorate within two or three days. For storage longer than three days, you should use the freezer. To freeze shellfish (other than lobster, mollusks, or crab), pack them, uncooked, into containers with enough shellfish juices or light brine to cover. To freeze lobster, mollusks and crab, cook in the desired manner, remove meat from the shell, cover with strained cooking liquids, wrap well and freeze for as long as three months.

SHERBET — Keep sherbet frozen.

SHERRY — See WINES AND SPIRITS.

SHITAKES — Usually available dried, these mushrooms can be stored in the dry pantry for a year.

SHOPPING LIST — Keep a shopping list posted in your pantry at all times, so that when you've run out of an item you can post it on the list immediately. Then when you sit down to make your grocery list, you won't have to make a complete inventory of your *Basic Pantry* to be assured of its proper supply. This way, you won't have those moments of frustration when you've returned from marketing and remember those few items you forgot to put on the list.

SHORTENING — Store shortening in airtight containers in the dry pantry. Substitution: Margarine or butter is a flavorful substitute for shortening in cooking.

SHRIMP — See SHELLFISH for storage information. Utilize the rich flavors contained within usually-discarded shells to make a sauce for the shrimp dish. After peeling the shrimp, place the shells in a small saucepan with either wine or water and lemon juice; sauté until the shells turn pink and aromas are released. Drain off the liquid and add it to your recipe or make a sauce to pour over the dish.

SHRIMP PASTE — You can substitute anchovy paste for shrimp paste listed in recipes or you may purchase this thick, pungent paste and keep it in the refrigerator pantry indefinitely.

SLICED MEATS — See COLD CUTS.

SNOW PEAS — Store unwashed snowpeas in the hydrator tub of the refrigerator for as long as two weeks. Blanche and freeze for as long as one year.

SOHO — See FISH.

SORGHUM STARCH — Store this product in an airtight container in the dry pantry.

SOUFFLÉS — You can store leftover soufflés in the refrigerator for three to five days. For longer storage, from three to six months, freezing is ideal.

Use leftover soufflés as fillings and stuffings for vegetables and fruits. For example, you can stuff cheese soufflé into a tomato and broil it, or you can use raspberry soufflé as a filling for crepes topped with fresh fruit.

SOUPS — See also STOCKS and STEW. Most soups are best if prepared ahead and allowed to "sit" for a day or two in the refrigerator. This allows the flavors to develop together richly. Soups freeze very well, except those with whole potatoes or potato pieces. You can expect a soup to preserve well for nine months in freezer storage, providing that before freezing, you have removed any fat layer which has arisen over the cooled surface. Save all liquids from cooking vegetables, poaching meats and fish, and draining canned vegetables; keep them in containers kept in your freezer pantry. All residual meat stocks, juices, and deglazing liquids can be kept in one container, marked "meat juices." Keep all vegetable-related liquids in another marked container; use these liquids as the basis for your soups. Have another container for fish and shellfish liquids, using it for chowders or ready made court bouillon. This can be thawed, used, and refrozen; it gets richer by the usage. See COURT BOUILLON.

SOUR CREAM — Store sour cream in the refrigerator until the expiration date on the package or no longer than two weeks from purchase. Substitutions: use 1 cup yogurt for 1 cup sour cream, or use 3/4 cup sour milk blended with 1/3 cup butter for 1 cup sour cream. Another substitution is 1 cup evaporated milk mixed with 1 tablespoon vinegar; allow to stand 5 minutes prior to use.

SOUR MILK — See MILK.

SOY FLOUR — Store soy flour in a labeled, airtight container in your refrigerator; it will keep for as long as six months; freezing will give it a storage life of one year.

SPAGHETTI — See PASTA.

SPAGHETTI SEASONING — Make your own seasoning for spaghetti sauce by mixing 2 tablespoons Italian seasoning, 2 teaspoons garlic powder, 2 teaspoons seasoning salt, 2 teaspoons salt, 1/2 teaspoon onion powder, 1 teaspoon pepper. This recipe makes approximately 1/3 cup seasoning. Store it in an airtight container and use 1 to 2 tablespoons in a sauce created to serve four to six people.

SPICES AND SPICED SEASONINGS — Keep them in dry, dark storage. Store them in whole form and grind them yourself, if possible. If purchasing ground spice, label and store it as long as one year.

## COMMON SPICES & THEIR USAGE

Allspice — cakes, pies, preserves, sauces, stews, beverages

Anise — See STAR ANISE.

Cajun — Creole dishes, meats, poultry, fish

Cardamom — Cakes, pastries, puddings, fruit, barbecue sauce, beverages

Cayenne — Mexican cookery, meats, sauces, eggs, vegetables, Italian foods

Cinnamon — baking, puddings, stewed fruits, sweet potatoes, beverages

Cloves — pork, pies, cakes, meatloaf, sauces, beets

Coriander — baking, custards, legume soups, pickling, egg dishes

Ginger — Chinese cookery, marinades, cakes, cookies, carrots, onions

Mace — game, baking, fish, vegetables, pickling

Nutmeg — egg dishes, baked products, soups, vegetables, poultry

Paprika — curry, appetizers, meatloaf, gravies, salad dressing

Pepper — all meat dishes, eggs, tomatoes, sauces, salads

Saffron — rice, sweetbreads, seafood, dumplings, poultry, veal

Star anise — Oriental meat dishes, game, lamb, liqueurs, jellies

Turmeric — creamed dishes and soups, marinades, seafood

## SPICED SEASONINGS

Cajun — meats, poultry, fish, pasta, casseroles

Chili Powder — Mexican cookery, cheese dishes, legumes, stews

Curry Powder — curried meats, eggs, cheese dishes, rice, pasta, vegetables

Five Spice Powder — Oriental cookery, casseroles, barbecue sauce; a combination of fennel, cloves, cinnamon, pepper and anise

Harissa — eastern foods, middle-eastern dishes, Italian cookery

Italian seasoning — Italian cookery, ground meat dishes, marinades, poultry

Lemon Pepper — fish, seafood, casseroles, breaded food

Poultry seasoning — all poultry dishes, vegetables, casseroles

Quatre Epices — French cookery, sauces, game, stew, paté

Seasoned Salt — vegetables, vegetable juices, meats, poultry, fish, soups, salads

Spaghetti seasoning — spaghetti sauce, pizza sauce, meatloaf

Taco seasoning - ground meat, salads, vegetables, meatloaf

MSG (monosodium glutamate) — Use sparingly as a flavor enhancer in meats and vegetable dishes

SPINACH — Store unwashed spinach in the hydrator tub of the refrigerator, either wrapped in toweling or in a brown bag. Sauté spinach in a little bacon fat to enhance flavor and reduce bitterness.

SPONGE CAKE — See CAKE.

SQUASH — Store assorted varieties of winter squash, such as acorn, at room temperature for as long as four months. Summer squash, such as zucchini, can be stored at room temperature for one or two weeks or unwashed in the hydrator tub for as long as three or four weeks. You can freeze squash as long as one year; slice and parboil or shred and sauté; then freeze.

SRIRACHA SAUCE — This Thai-style pepper sauce can be stored in the dry pantry.

STAR ANISE — See SPICES AND SPICED SEASONINGS.

STARCHES — See THICKENERS.

STEAK — See specific meat, such as beef, pork or salmon.

STEM GINGER — This product is cooked knobs of peeled ginger, preserved in syrup; store it in the dry pantry.

STEW — After skimming off any fat that settles on top, store fresh-made stew, covered, in the refrigerator for as long as one week. Stew can be frozen successfully for as long as nine months, but if you make stew for freezing, don't add potatoes and other chunks of fresh vegetables until after thawing; freezing can affect the firm texture of cooked vegetables and potatoes.

STEWED FRUIT — You can store stewed fruit, well sealed, in the refrigerator for as long as one or two weeks. Freezer life is one year.

STOCK (consommé) — Beef, veal, poultry, fish, seafood and vegetable stock can be refrigerated for weeks, providing you boil the stock for 10 minutes every three days. A less time consuming way of storage is to freeze stocks (for as long as six months) in dated containers; an alternative is to use ice cube trays to freeze the stock, then store the cubes in labeled and dated plastic bags. If you wish to prepare a meat stock for use within eight or ten days, you do not need to freeze or boil every three days. Just allow the surface fat to remain on top during refrigeration to provide an airtight seal, as well as act as a natural preservative. Use the stock within ten days. If you boil stocks frequently it intensifies the flavor; replace evaporated water with fluids to equal the amount of stock needed. You may wish to enhance canned stock or consommé by bringing it to a boil and simmering it with green herbs and roasted vegetables. Strain before use, so that you can reserve the liquids in your freezer container.

STRAWBERRIES — See BERRIES.

STRING BEANS — See BEANS AND LEGUMES.

STUFFING (poultry dressing) — Keep leftover stuffing in airtight containers in the refrigerator, no longer than three to five days. It can be frozen for three months. Do *not* freeze or store any stuffing with the poultry cavity. Heat frozen stuffing directly from the freezer in a moderate oven for 20 or 25 minutes.

SUBSTITUTIONS — For possible substitution ideas, refer either to the item needed or an item which you have available.

SUGAR — Store sugar (granulated, superfine, brown or confectioner's) indefinitely in airtight containers in your dry pantry. If sugars (other than confectioner's) become hard or chunky during storage, heat in a moderate oven for a few minutes, until sugar softens. You can soften brown sugar in the microwave oven because of its higher moisture content.

See also HONEY, PRALINE POWDER, POWDERED SUGAR, CINNAMON SUGAR, VANILLA SUGAR, MOLASSES.

SUN DRIED TOMATOES — These dried plum tomatoes are usually packed in oil, but they also are available dry.

SWEETBREADS — This delicate meat is highly perishable; store it in the refrigerator only one day after purchase.

SWEET POTATOES — Store sweet potatoes in the dry pantry, for no longer than three to five days from purchase. Do not freeze raw sweet potatoes; even cooked or baked sweet potatoes' texture is adversely affected during freezing, though their use in cooking or baking is fine.

SWISS CHARD — Chard can be stored and cooked as spinach, although chard is tougher.

SYRUP — See also MAPLE SYRUP.

Corn Syrup (light and dark) — Store it in the dry pantry for as long as one to three years.

Italian Syrup — Flavored syrups used in beverage making. Store in dry pantry indefinitely.

Pancake Syrup — Store pancake syrup at room temperature or in the refrigerator, although refrigeration allows crystallization. To reduce crystallization in homemade syrup, add a pinch of cream of tartar to each cup of sugar used.

Sugar Syrup — This is used for canning fruits, and the sugar syrup should be made only immediately before preparing the fruit. No storage should occur, although leftover syrup can be stored for a few days in the dry pantry, if ascorbic acid hasn't been added.
See Appendix for syrup mixtures.

### -T-

TABLE FATS — butter, margarine, lard, shortening. Store these as individually indicated.

TACO CHIPS — Store unopened taco chips in the dry pantry for as long as three months; once they've been opened they'll last one week in the dry pantry.

TACO SEASONING — Add this pre-made seasoning to 1 pound ground beef which has been sautéed with 1 chopped onion: 1 1/2 teaspoons chili powder, 1 teaspoon garlic salt, 1/2 teaspoon each oregano and paprika, 1/4 teaspoon each rosemary, cumin and black pepper. Triple the recipe and store in a small, airtight container in your spice cupboard for sprinkling on refried beans and canned chili and for making enchiladas.

TACO SHELLS — You can store unopened taco shells in the dry pantry for three months; opened, they will last for one week.

TAMARIND — This food product comes in many forms, with tamarind concentrate having the most diversified uses. Tamarind water is made from soaking the concentrate in water for 10 minutes; the resulting liquid is used in many recipes. Store on the dry pantry shelf until opened, then refrigerate for as long as a year.

TAPIOCA — Store this product in the dry pantry indefinitely.

TAPIOCA FLOUR — Store this flour in an airtight container in the refrigerator for long term storage. See THICKENERS.

TARO (Dasheen) — This root vegetable should be stored in the hydrator tub for no longer than two weeks.

TARRAGON — See HERBS & HERBAL SEASONINGS.

TARTAR SAUCE — Keep bottled tartar sauce on the dry pantry shelf until opened, then refrigerate for as long as six months. If you make your own fresh tartar sauce, it will keep for a week in an airtight container in your refrigerator. Simply mix 1/2 cup mayonnaise with 1 tablespoon sweet pickle relish and 1 teaspoon lemon juice.

TEA — Keep tea in airtight jars; its potency will diminish after a year. Utilize extra tea by freezing it in cubes for cooling iced tea drinks without diluting the beverage.

TERRINES — Fresh terrines can be refrigerated for five days if they are sealed with a layer of aspic or meat jelly. Freeze them for as long as three months.

THICKENERS — Arrowroot, cornstarch, potato starch (flour), all-purpose flour, instant flour, tapioca starch, rice and barley flour are all suitable thickeners in cooking and baking. Most, with the exception of tapioca and potato flours, can be stored safely in airtight containers in your dry pantry indefinitely. (Tapioca and potato starch keep best in sealed containers placed in the refrigerator, for as long as one year.) Once prepared into a slurry, roux, panada, or pearls, these thickening agents can be stored for instant use in your refrigerator for a month. Use cornstarch or arrowroot if you wish your final sauce to be translucent. Two tablespoons flour are equivalent to 1 tablespoon cornstarch in thickening power. Arrowroot is even more potent than cornstarch; use slightly less arrowroot in measuring equivalents of cornstarch to flour. Potato starch is slightly less thickening than cornstarch; use a bit more in equivalents from cornstarch to flour. Follow package directions for tapioca.

THYME — See HERBS AND HERBAL SEASONINGS.

TIMBALES — Leftover formed foods such as timbales can be refrigerated for approximately three days, if they are well wrapped. Freezing provides better storage — as long as three months — ideally, enclosed with gravy or sauce.

TOFFEE — Store toffee in the dry pantry for no longer than one year.

TOFU — This soy curd can be stored in water in the refrigerator, for one week or according to the date on the package. The water should be changed daily.

TOMATO JUICE — Fresh or canned tomato juice can be stored in plastic or glass containers in the refrigerator for as long as two weeks. You can make your own tomato juice for use in cooking by adding 1/2 cup water to 1/2 cup tomato sauce; if a larger quantity is needed, for a dish such as stew, add three 6 oz. cans cold water to one 6 oz. can tomato paste, plus 1 teaspoon salt.

TOMATO PASTE — Store canned tomato paste in the dry pantry for as long as two years. Once opened, either canned or fresh-made tomato paste must be frozen in small containers for long term storage (six to eight months) or refrigerated in glass or plastic for no longer than two weeks. You can substitute tomato paste for many tomato preparations, e.g., juice, puree and sauce. However, if you need a substitute for tomato paste in cooking, simply add 2 tablespoons flour to 1 cup tomato sauce, stir and heat to the bubbly stage; use this as you would tomato paste.

TOMATO SAUCE — Store this as you would tomato paste. Use tomato sauce as a substitute for tomato soup in recipes. As a substitute for tomato sauce, you can use a 6 oz. can of tomato paste with 3/4 cup water to equal 1 1/2 cups sauce.

TOMATO PUREE — Fresh tomato puree must be kept in a glass or plastic container in the refrigerator, for no longer than two weeks. Freeze in small containers for as long as six months. As a substitute for tomato puree, use a 6 oz. can tomato paste with 1 can water, then season.

TOMATOES — Store ripe tomatoes in the refrigerator for no longer than one week. Before serving sliced, raw tomatoes, allow them to come to room temperature for the best flavor. Unripe tomatoes can be stored in the dry pantry until they are ripe, then moved to the refrigerator. Tomatoes can be frozen, but the texture is greatly affected. See BLANCHING for instructions. If you need a substitute for fresh tomatoes in cooking, you can use canned, drained tomatoes, though the texture may affect the final appearance of the dish.

TOMATILLOS — You may store this vegetable in the dry pantry for no longer than two weeks.

TONGUE — Store fresh tongue in the refrigerator for no longer than three days after purchase. Freeze beef tongue, after slicing or cutting into stew meat sizes, for as long as three to six months.

TOPPINGS — See specific types, such as CHEESECAKE TOPPING, COOKIES and CAKES.

TORTILLAS — Flour and corn tortillas can be stored for weeks in the refrigerator and as long as one year in the freezer.

TREACLE — See MOLASSES.

TROUT — See FISH.

TRUFFLES — These fungi are very delicate; fresh truffles should be used within one week. Store them in the refrigerator.

TUNA — Fresh tuna may be stored, well wrapped, for no longer than three to five days in the refrigerator. See FISH for freezing ideas. Canned tuna is ideal to keep around for quick meals; once opened, refrigerate it and use it within three days.

TURKEY—See POULTRY. Buy extra whole turkeys during peak season and freeze, to save on cost per pound.

TURMERIC — See SPICES AND SPICED SEASONINGS.

TURNIPS — Store turnips in the hydrator tub of your refrigerator for no longer than two weeks. Use them as you would carrots in recipes. (Slightly sweeter, rutabagas are yellow turnips.)

TURTLE BEANS — See BLACK BEANS.

## -U-

UNLEAVENED BREADS — Matzo, pita bread, and corn and flour tortillas are examples of unleavened breads. They may be stored in the dry pantry for one week. To refrigerate, wrap well in plastic or place in an airtight container for as long as one month. They may be frozen for six months.

## -V-

VANILLA — To prevent drying out, store vanilla pods in small, airtight containers in the dry pantry. You *can* also keep a pod in granulated or superfine sugar in large containers, provided that they are airtight. Use the sugar in baking and replace the amount of sugar taken out of the storage container. Vanilla powder has a shelf life of approximately one year; sprinkle on cappucino or you *can* use it in recipes as you would liquid extract, but add it to dry ingredients. Vanilla extract, either true or imitation, will keep for two years with valid potency; you can use more vanilla extract than the amount listed in a recipe — up to twice as much, as desired for more intense flavor.

VANILLA SUGAR — Keep two or three cups of superfine or granulated sugar in a labeled, airtight container with a vanilla pod (bean). Use it in dessert making whenever sugar is listed in the recipe.

VARIETY MEATS — See KIDNEYS, LIVER, SWEETBREADS, TONGUE and COLD CUTS.

VEAL — Store fresh veal, well wrapped, in the refrigerator for no longer than three days. For longer storage, veal can be frozen for six months. This delicate meat shouldn't be stored for longer periods of time, since flavor and moisture can be lost easily.

VEGETABLES — See specific kinds for storage information.

## HINTS FOR PRESERVING VEGETABLE FLAVOR AND NUTRITION

1. Most vegetables should not be washed prior to storing.

2. Use or reserve all liquids with which vegetables come in contact during steaming, sautéing or boiling. Reduce for easier storage. Reserved liquid can be used to make stocks and stews or to serve as a base for a vegetable or meat sauce. Nutrients and vitamins are in the liquids.

3. Except for potatoes, do not salt vegetables during cooking; use sugar, if necessary, to bring out flavors.

4. As a rule, fresh vegetables begin to lose nutrients within one or two weeks; use them as quickly as possible.

5. Always try to use vegetable stock or meat stocks in sautéing or steaming fresh vegetables. This greatly enhances the flavor of the vegetable, as well as increasing the nutritive value and flavor of the stock.

6. Use lots of herbs — either fresh or dried — while cooking vegetables. See HERBS AND HERBAL SEASONINGS.

7. Do not add baking soda to vegetables.

8. Reserve *all* liquids from canned vegetables and keep them in your freezer in a marked container for use in creating such things as soups, stocks, sauces and gravies.

VEGETABLE CURLS — These decorative vegetables are kept in water in the refrigerator; they can provide an appetizing color to any dish to which you care to add them. Use a vegetable peeler to cut thin strips of carrot or slice down small 1-inch strips on the ends of celery sticks. See individual headings for more detail.

VEGETABLE OILS — Store vegetable oils in a dark, cool cupboard or in dark bottles; they'll keep for as long as a year, after opening.

VEGETABLE SHORTENING — Store shortening, well covered, in a cool place as long as one year after opening.

VICHYSSOISE — See SOUPS.

VINEGAR — This stable liquid can be stored for years in the dry pantry. Reserve leftover wines or wine that has become bitter from standing; it can be added to vinegar to make your own red or white wine vinegar. Use a small amount of cider vinegar in water to use as a quick dip for sliced fruits that darken quickly; allowing them to retain their natural color before serving or cooking.

VINAIGRETTE — Store commercial salad dressing/marinade in the refrigerator as long as one year, use fresh vinaigrette immediately.

VITAMINS — Store vitamins in a dark cupboard, away from heat and/or moisture.

VODKA — See Chapter 9, "A Larder of Extracts, Liqueurs and Spirits."

## -W-

WAFFLES — You may store leftover waffles for three days in the refrigerator. For longer storage, freeze waffles between layers of waxed paper and cover the entire package with plastic wrap; they'll keep for three months.

WALNUTS — See NUTS.

WATER — Keep a supply of distilled, purified and pure drinking water in your dry pantry for emergencies and household use.

WATER CHESTNUTS — Cover both fresh, peeled water chestnuts and opened, canned ones with water; they'll store in the refrigerator for one week. Add them to potato salads for a new taste sensation, or try using sliced fresh water chestnuts and a mint sprig for a palate cleanser.

WATERCRESS — See SALAD GREENS.

WATERCRESS BUTTERBALLS — See HERBAL BUTTERBALLS. Keep available in the freezer a supply of watercress butterballs for a quick and flavorful topping for broiled or grilled meats, poultry, and fish.

WATERMELON — Uncut watermelon can be stored for weeks in the dry pantry. Sliced watermelon, well covered, will keep on the bottom shelf of the refrigerator for two weeks.

WAX BEANS — See BEANS.

WHEAT — See FLOUR and WHOLE WHEAT.

WHIPPED TOPPING — Commercial whipped topping can be stored in the refrigerator until the expiration date or until 1 1/2 weeks after the purchase date. Whipped, fresh cream, has a refrigerator life of only one week, due to its high fat content. Both commercial and fresh whipped toppings (except for canned carbonated) can be successfully frozen for as long as three months.

WHITE CANNELLINI BEANS — Store dried beans in the pantry for as long as one year. Canned beans that have been opened can be kept in a fresh container in the refrigerator for two weeks. You may freeze cooked beans if necessary, but freezing can affect texture after thawing.

WHOLE WHEAT BERRIES — Store whole wheat in an airtight container in the refrigerator for long storage — one or two years. It can be stored, tightly sealed, in the dry pantry for a month.

WINES — Store all unopened wines on their sides, away from temperature extremes. Ideally, 55° to 60° F. Opened wines should be consumed within one or two days. If the container is well sealed, it can retain freshness longer. Use any wines that are flat, in cooking. You can refrigerate them at this point. Wines which have soured or are flat can be added to vinegar to make either homemade red or white wine vinegar. When a recipe calls for wine, if the amount is something like 1/2 cup red or 1/2 cup white wine, you can substitute 1/4 cup of any acidic fruit juice — like sour grape or apple juice — combined with 1/4 cup water to equal the necessary liquid. For use in cooking and baking, keep a supply of the following:

*White Wine* — dry, such as white table wine or Chardonnay, or sweet, such as Vouvray or Riesling

*Rosé* — such as white Zinfandel or blush wine

*Sherry* — dry, such as Amontadillo, for vegetable and meat sauces, and sweet, such as Amoroso or cream, for desserts and sauces

*Port* — such as Madeira, Marsala, Malaga

*Aperitifs* — dry, red, or sweet vermouth

*Sparkling Wines/Champagnes* — blanc de blanc or rosé

WORCESTERSHIRE SAUCE — Store this product in the dry pantry for as long as two years, or according to directions on the bottle. Substitutions: Use either diluted steak sauce (1 to 1) or soy sauce.

## -Y-

YAMS — Keep yams in the dry pantry for no longer than three to five days after purchase. Refrigerate baked yams no longer than three days, for they will begin to weep. It is better to purée leftover yams and freeze them, for as long as six months. Use puréed yams, either fresh or frozen, as a substitute for carrots in carrot cake and muffins and as a substitute for pumpkin in any recipe.

YEAST — Keep granulated and cake yeast in the refrigerator for the best long term storage. Check the potency of yeast by placing a small amount (1/2 teaspoon) of yeast in 1/4 cup warm water. This should bubble within 5 or 10 minutes if the yeast is active. You can freeze yeast.

YELLOW BEAN PASTE — Keep opened jars of paste/sauce in the refrigerator for as long as one year.

YOGURT — Store commercial yogurt in the refrigerator until the expiration date on the package. Store fresh-made yogurt no longer than five days. Frozen yogurt must be kept frozen; do not refreeze if thawed.

YORKSHIRE PUDDING — Leftover puddings can be refrigerated for one week; freezing is not recommended.

## -Z-

ZEST — See specific zest, such as LEMON or ORANGE.

ZUCCHINI — See SQUASH.

# APPENDIX:
# PANTRY CHARTS & TABLES

### *TABLE I.*
### *MASTER SHOPPING LIST*

Use this list to enable you to make out your own shopping lists in an effective shopping order.

1. Produce (vegetables and fruits)

2. Dry Goods
   Flours & grains
   Rice
   Pasta
   Starches
   Sugars
   Oils & Fats
   Vinegars
   Herbs and spices
   Cooking & baking essentials
   Beverages, wines, and spirits
   Misc. stored foods (cans or bottles)
   > Vegetables
   > Fruits
   > Meats
   > Soups
   > Legumes
   > Fish
   > Seafood

3. Fresh meats, poultry and seafood

4. Dairy

5. Freezer items

## TABLE II.
## TIMETABLE FOR BLANCHING VEGETABLES AND FRUITS PRIOR TO FREEZING

Note: For each pound of prepared vegetable, use at least 1 gallon boiling water. After heating for the specified time, cool promptly in cold water and drain.

| Vegetable | Heated in Boiling Water |
|---|---|
| Apples, sliced | 60 seconds |
| Asparagus, small stalks | 2 minutes |
|    Medium stalks | 3 minutes |
|    Large stalks | 4 minutes |
| Beans, green or wax | 3 minutes |
| Beans, lima, small beans or pods | 2 minutes |
| Broccoli, flowerets | 3 minutes |
| Brussels sprouts, small heads | 3 minutes |
|    Medium heads | 4 minutes |
|    Large heads | 5 minutes |
| Cabbage, coarse shreds or thin wedges | 1 1/2 min. |
| Carrots, whole carrots, small | 5 minutes |
|    Diced, sliced, strips | 2 minutes |
| Corn, sweet, on the cob Small ears (1 1/4" or less in dia.) | 7 minutes |
|    Medium ears (1 1/4" - 1 1/2") | 9 minutes |
|    Large ears (over 1 1/2" in dia.) | 11 minutes |
|    Whole kernel (off cob) | 2 min. |
| Greens, beet, chard, kale, mustard, spinach, turnip | 2 minutes |
|    Collards | 3 minutes |
| Kohlrabi, 1/2" cubes | 1 minute |
| Okra, small pods | 3 minutes |
|    Large pods | 4 minutes |
| Parsnips, 1/2" cubes or slices | 2 minutes |
| Peaches | 30 - 45 seconds |
| Peas, black-eyed | 2 minutes |
| Peas, green | 1 1/2 min. |

```
Peppers, halves  . . . . . . . . . . . . . . . . 3 minutes
       Slices  . . . . . . . . . . . . . . . . . . . . 2 minutes
Pumpkin  . . . . . . . . . . . . . . . . . . . . . . Until soft
Rutabagas, 1/2" cubes  . . . . . . . . . . . 2 minutes
Squash, summer, 1/2" slices  . . . . . . . 3 minutes
       Winter  . . . . . . . . . . . . . . . . . . . . until soft
Tomatoes  . . . . . . . . . . . . . . . . . . . . . 5 - 10 min.
Turnips, 1/2" cubes  . . . . . . . . . . . . . . 2 minutes
Zucchini, shredded  . . . . . . . . . . . . . . 1 minute
```

## TABLE III.
## FREEZER STORAGE TIMES

| Food for Freezing | Storage Time (in mos.) at 0° F |
|---|---|

**Baked goods**
```
      Angel food & chiffon cakes  . . . . . . . . . . 2
      Breads  &  rolls,  prebaked  . . . . . . . . . . . 3
      Cakes & pound cakes, prebaked   . . . 4 - 8
      Cake batter  . . . . . . . . . . . . . . . . . . . . . . 3
      Doughnuts & pastries  . . . . . . . . . . . . . . 3
      Fruit pies, unbaked  . . . . . . . . . . . . . . . . 8
      Sweet rolls & coffee cakes  . . . . . . . . . . 2
      Yeast doughs &
            unbaked pie shells  . . . . . . . . . . . . 2
      Casseroles (generally)  . . . . . . . . . . . . 3 - 6
```
**Dairy**
```
      Butter & margarine  . . . . . . . . . . . . . . . . 2
      Cheese (hard & soft)  . . . . . . . . . . . . . 3 - 6
      Cream (light & whipping)   . . . . . . . . . 3 - 6
      Eggs  . . . . . . . . . . . . . . . . . . . . . . . . . . . . 4
      Milk  . . . . . . . . . . . . . . . . . . . . . . . . . . . . 3
```
**Fish, shellfish & seafoods**
```
      Fish fillets (high fat content)  . . . . . . . . . 3
      Fish fillets (low fat content)  . . . . . . . . . . 6
      Fried fish & seafoods  . . . . . . . . . . . . . . 3
      Fish casseroles &
            cooked fish dishes   . . . . . . . . . . . 3
      Crabmeat, clams, shucked oysters  . . . . 3
      Shrimp  . . . . . . . . . . . . . . . . . . . . . . . 6 - 12
      Fish & seafood liquids  . . . . . . . . . . . . . 3
```

Frozen desserts
 Ice creams ........................1
 Sherbet ...........................1
 Packaged ice cream bars ...........1
 Frozen yogurt .....................1
 Fruit pie filling .................. 6 - 8
 Fruits, fruit juice
   concentrates, fruit liquids ... 9 - 12

Meats (fresh unless otherwise noted)
 Beef — Hamburger,
   ground round,
   or stew meats ............ 3 - 4
   Roasts & steaks .......... 12
 Cured meats ......................1
 Lamb — Ground or stew meat ... 3 - 4
   Chops or steaks ...........4
   Roasts, whole legs ..........9
 Meat dinners & dishes,
   precooked .............. 2 - 3
 Meat Stocks ......................6
 Pork — Ground & sausage ......... 1 - 2
   Chops & steaks ...........4
   Roasts .................8
   Cured ...................2
 Veal — Cutlets, chops, & roasts .......9

Poultry (fresh unless otherwise noted)
 Chicken, cut-up .................. 6 - 9
 Chicken, whole .................. 9 - 12
 Chicken stock, poultry liquids .........6
 Cooked poultry dishes
   & casseroles ............ 3 - 6
 Cornish hens ................... 6 - 12
 Ducks & geese, whole ..............6
 Fried chicken ....................4
 Turkey, cut-up ....................6
 Turkey, whole ................... 12

Nuts & Nut meats .................. 12 - 14

Vegetables, dishes & casseroles ..........6

Vegetables, plain .................... 12

Vegetable liquids .....................6

## TABLE IV.
## COMMON MEASURES AND EQUIVALENTS

Tablespoon

1 Tbsp. = 3 tsp.
7/8 Tbsp. = 2 1/2 tsp.
3/4 Tbsp. = 2 1/4 tsp.
2/3 Tbsp. = 2 tsp.
5/8 Tbsp. = 1 7/8 tsp.
1/2 Tbsp. = 1 1/2 tsp.
3/8 Tbsp. = 1 1/8 tsp.
1/3 Tbsp. = 1 tsp.
1/4 Tbsp. = 3/4 tsp.

Pint

1 pt. = 2 c.
7/8 pt. = 1 3/4 c.
3/4 pt. = 1 1/2 c.
2/3 pt. = 1 1/3 c.
5/8 pt. = 1 1/4 c.
1/2 pt. = 1 c.
3/8 pt. = 3/4 c.
1/3 pt. = 2/3 c.
1/4 pt. = 1/2 c.
1/8 pt. = 1/4 c.
1/16 pt. = 2 Tbsp.

Gallon

1 gal. = 4 qt.
7/8 gal. = 3 1/2 qt.
3/4 gal. = 3 qt.
2/3 gal. = 10 2/3 c.
5/8 gal. = 5 pt.
1/2 gal. = 2 qt.
3/8 gal. = 3 pt.
1/3 gal. = 5 1/3 c.
1/4 gal. = 1 qt.
1/8 gal. = 1 pt.
1/16 gal. = 1 c.

Cup

1 c. = 16 Tbsp.
7/8 c. = 14 Tbsp.
3/4 c. = 12 Tbsp.
2/3 c. = 10 2/3 Tbsp.
5/8 c. = 10 Tbsp.
1/2 c. = 8 Tbsp.
3/8 c. = 6 Tbsp.
1/3 c. = 5 1/3 Tbsp.
1/4 c. = 4 Tbsp.
1/8 c. = 2 Tbsp.
1/16 c. = 1 Tbsp.

Quart

1 qt. = 2 pt.
7/8 qt. = 3 1/2 c.
3/4 qt. = 3 c.
2/3 qt. = 2 2/3 c.
5/8 qt. = 2 1/2 c.
1/2 qt. = 1 pt.
3/8 qt. = 1 1/2 c.
1/3 qt. = 1 1/3 c.
1/4 qt. = 1 c.
1/8 qt. = 1/2 c.
1/16 qt. = 1/4 c.

Pound

1 lb. = 16 oz.
7/8 lb. = 14 oz.
3/4 lb. = 12 oz.
2/3 lb. = 10 2/3 oz.
5/8 lb. = 10 oz.
1/2 lb. = 8 oz.
3/8 lb. = 6 oz.
1/3 lb. = 5 1/3 oz.
1/4 lb. = 4 oz.
1/8 lb. = 2 oz.
1/16 lb. = 1 oz.

## TABLE V.
## METRIC CONVERSIONS

1 oz. = 28 gms.

1 cup = 1/4 liter

1 pt. = 1/2 liter

1 qt. = .946 liter

1 lb. = 450 gms.

2.2 lb. = 1 kilogram

## TABLE VI.
## OVEN TEMPERATURES (Fahrenheit)

250° - 275° - Very slow oven.

300° - 325° - Slow oven.

350° - 375° - Moderate oven.

400° - 425° - Hot oven.

450° - 475° - Very hot oven.

500° - 525° - Extremely hot.

## TABLE VII.
## SUGAR SYRUP FOR
## COOKING AND PRESERVING

In making syrups, heat the indicated amount of sugar and water needed in a heavy saucepan, just until the sugar dissolves. Use 1 to 1 1/2 cups warm syrup for each quart of fruit to be canned; use 1/2 to 2/3 cup cooked syrup per pint of fruit which you plan to freeze.

| Syrup | Density | Sugar | Water | Yield |
|---|---|---|---|---|
| Very thin............ | 1 | 4 | | $4\,^3/_4$ |
| Thin.................. | 4 | 5 | | |
| Medium............. | 3 | 4 | | $5\,^1/_2$ |
| Heavy............... | $4\,^3/_4$ | 4 | | $6\,^1/_2$ |
| Very heavy........ | 7 | 4 | | $7\,^3/_4$ |
| Homemade pancake syrup.......... | 8 | 4 | | $8\,^1/_4$ |

## TABLE VIII.
## BASIC PANTRY CHECKLIST
*(Including perishables: store in refrigerator)*

### Miscellaneous Grains
□ Unbleached
  White Flour
□ All-Purpose Flour
□ Whole Wheat Flour
□ Self Rising Flour
□ Cake Flour
□ Pastry Flour
□ Regular Oats
□ Instant Oats
□ Yellow Cornmeal
□ Wheat Germ
□ Bran
□ Grits (regional)
□ Farina
□ Wheat Flakes
□ Preferred Hot Cereals

### Prepared Mixes
□ Biscuit Mix
□ Pancake Mix
□ Cornbread Mix

### Rices
□ Instant or Converted
□ Long Grain White
□ Brown Rice

### Pasta
□ Spaghetti
□ Linguini
□ Wide Egg Noodles
□ Fettucini
□ Lasagna
□ Ravioli
□ Macaroni
□ Tortellini
□ Spinach Noodles

### Starches & Thickening Agents
□ Cornstarch
□ Tapioca Starch
□ Unflavored Gelatin

### Sweetening Agents
□ Granulated Sugar
□ Superfine Sugar
□ Confectioner's Sugar
□ Light Brown Sugar
□ Dark Brown Sugar
□ Honey
□ Molasses
□ Light Corn Syrup
□ Dark Corn Syrup
□ Pancake Syrup
□ Artificial Sweeteners

### Oils & Fats
□ Virgin Olive Oil
□ Extra Virgin Olive Oil
□ Corn Oil
□ Safflower or
  Vegetable Oil
□ Peanut Oil
□ Vegetable Oil Spray
□ Lard
□ Shortening
□ Butter or Margarine

### Vinegars
□ White Distilled
□ Cider Vinegar
□ Red Wine Vinegar
□ Rice Vinegar

## Dried Herbs
- ☐ Basil
- ☐ Bay Leaves
- ☐ Celery Seed
- ☐ Chives
- ☐ Dill Weed
- ☐ Marjoram
- ☐ Oregano
- ☐ Parsley Flakes
- ☐ Rosemary
- ☐ Sage
- ☐ Savory
- ☐ Thyme

## Spices
- ☐ Allspice
- ☐ Cardamom
- ☐ Cayenne
- ☐ Chili Powder
- ☐ Cinnamon, Ground
- ☐ Cinnamon Sticks
- ☐ Cloves, Whole
- ☐ Cloves, Ground
- ☐ Curry
- ☐ Ginger, Ground
- ☐ Mace
- ☐ Mustard, Dry
- ☐ Nutmeg, Whole
- ☐ Nutmeg, Grated
- ☐ Paprika
- ☐ Pepper, Ground
- ☐ Pepper, Whole
- ☐ White Pepper
- ☐ Lemon Pepper

## Seasonings & Condiments
- ☐ Granulated Salt
- ☐ Coarse Salt
- ☐ Seasoning Salt
- ☐ Garlic Salt
- ☐ Garlic Powder
- ☐ Accent Flavor Enhancer
- ☐ MSG
- ☐ Mayonnaise
- ☐ Ketchup
- ☐ Yellow Mustard
- ☐ Dijon Mustard
- ☐ Assorted Salad Dressings
- ☐ Soy Sauce
- ☐ Hot Sauce
- ☐ Chili Sauce
- ☐ Teriyaki Sauce
- ☐ Barbecue Sauce
- ☐ Worcestershire Sauce
- ☐ Tartar Sauce
- ☐ Horseradish
- ☐ Assorted Pickles and Relishes
- ☐ Packaged Gravy Mixes
- ☐ Packaged Sauce Mixes

## Essentials for Preparing Foods
- ☐ Beef Stock
- ☐ Chicken Stock
- ☐ Vegetable Stock
- ☐ Fish Stock
- ☐ Clam Juice
- ☐ Tomato Paste
- ☐ Tomato Sauce
- ☐ Tomato Juice
- ☐ Vegetable Juice
- ☐ Enchilada Sauce
- ☐ Assorted Marinara
- ☐ Cranberry Sauce, Gel
- ☐ Cranberry Sauce, Whole Berry
- ☐ Assorted Dried Fruits

- ☐ Green Chilies
- ☐ Dried Onion Flakes
- ☐ Bacon Bits
- ☐ Fresh Bread
- ☐ Poultry Stuffing
- ☐ Fine Bread Crumbs
- ☐ Prepared Soups
- ☐ Meat Tenderizer

*Essentials for*
*Breads & Desserts*
- ☐ Active Dry Yeast
- ☐ Baking Powder
- ☐ Baking Soda
- ☐ Cream of Tartar
- ☐ Sweetened
  Condensed Milk
- ☐ Evaporated Milk
- ☐ Nonfat Dry Milk
- ☐ Coffee Granules
- ☐ Bitter Chocolate
- ☐ Semi-sweet Chocolate
- ☐ White Chocolate
- ☐ Cocoa Powder
- ☐ Chocolate Chips
- ☐ Peanut Butter
- ☐ Jams or Jellies
- ☐ Coconut, Flaked
- ☐ Food Coloring
- ☐ Popcorn

*Extracts*
- ☐ Almond
- ☐ Cherry
- ☐ Chocolate
- ☐ Lemon
- ☐ Maple
- ☐ Mint
- ☐ Orange
- ☐ Rum
- ☐ Vanilla

*Canned Goods*
- ☐ Chicken
- ☐ Turkey
- ☐ Ham
- ☐ Corned Beef Hash
- ☐ Tuna
- ☐ Crab
- ☐ Shrimp
- ☐ Clams
- ☐ Sardines
- ☐ Creamed Corn
- ☐ Kernel Corn
- ☐ Carrots
- ☐ Peas
- ☐ Leaf Spinach
- ☐ Green Beans
- ☐ Potatoes
- ☐ Yams
- ☐ Beets
- ☐ Mushrooms
- ☐ Unsalted Stewed
  Tomatoes
- ☐ Unsalted Whole
  Tomatoes
- ☐ Pimentos
- ☐ Green Stuffed Olives
- ☐ Black Pitted Olives
- ☐ Sauerkraut
- ☐ Peaches
- ☐ Pears
- ☐ Sliced Pineapple
- ☐ Small Chunk
  Pineapple
- ☐ Fruit Cocktail
- ☐ Mandarin Oranges
- ☐ Cherries
- ☐ Assorted Pie Fillings

### Nuts and Seeds
- ☐ Peanuts
- ☐ Whole Almonds
- ☐ Sliced Almonds
- ☐ Slivered Almonds
- ☐ Cashews
- ☐ Walnuts
- ☐ Pecans
- ☐ Sunflower Seeds

### Canned & Dried Legumes
- ☐ Navy Beans
- ☐ Pinto Beans
- ☐ Kidney Beans
- ☐ Garbanzo Beans
- ☐ Lentils
- ☐ Split Green Peas

### Dairy Products
- ☐ Cheddar Cheese
- ☐ Jack Cheese
- ☐ Swiss Cheese
- ☐ Cream Cheese
- ☐ Cottage Cheese
- ☐ Ricotta Cheese
- ☐ Parmesan or
     Romano Cheese
- ☐ Milk
- ☐ Cream
- ☐ Sour Cream
- ☐ Sweet Cream Butter
- ☐ Eggs

### Meats & Fish
- ☐ Ground beef
- ☐ Ground Pork
- ☐ White Fish Fillets
- ☐ Poultry cuts

### Vegetables
- ☐ Carrots
- ☐ Celery
- ☐ Salad Greens
- ☐ Tomatoes
- ☐ Green Onions
- ☐ Garlic
- ☐ Potatoes
- ☐ Broccoli
- ☐ Cauliflower
- ☐ Spinach
- ☐ Parsley

### Fruits
- ☐ Apples
- ☐ Bananas
- ☐ Grapes
- ☐ Oranges
- ☐ Grapefruit
- ☐ Lemon
- ☐ Lime

### Cooking Wines & Spirits
- ☐ Dry White Wine
- ☐ Dry Red Wine
- ☐ Marsala
- ☐ Dry Sherry
- ☐ Sweet Sherry
- ☐ Rum
- ☐ Assorted Liqueurs

### Beverages
- ☐ Milk
- ☐ Fruit Juice
- ☐ Soda Pop
- ☐ Mineral Water
- ☐ Club Soda
- ☐ Tonic Water
- ☐ Purified Water
- ☐ Tea
- ☐ Coffee

# INDEX

Additional copies of
PALATABLE PANTRIES AND LAVISH LARDERS
by Rhonda M. Mircovich, may be ordered
by sending a check or money order
for $17.95 postpaid for each copy to:

DISTINCTIVE PUBLISHING CORP.
P.O. Box 17868
Plantation FL 33318-7868
(305) 975-2413

Quantity discounts are also available
from the publisher.